RENAISSANCE LITERATURE AND CULTURE

INTRODUCTIONS TO BRITISH LITERATURE AND CULTURE SERIES

Introductions to British Literature and Culture are practical guides to key literary periods. Guides in the series are designed to help introduce a new module or area of study, providing concise information on the historical, literary and critical contexts and acting as an initial map of the knowledge needed to study the literature and culture of a specific period. Each guide includes an overview of the historical period, intellectual contexts, major genres, critical approaches and a guide to original research and resource materials in the area, enabling students to progress confidently to further study.

FORTHCOMING TITLES

Medieval Literature and Culture by Andrew Galloway

Seventeenth-Century Literature and Culture by Jim Daems

Eighteenth-Century Literature and Culture by Paul Goring

Victorian Literature and Culture by Maureen Moran

Romanticism by Sharon Ruston

Modernism by Leigh Wilson

Contemporary British Literature and Culture by Sean Matthews

RENAISSANCE LITERATURE AND CULTURE

Lisa Hopkins and Matthew Steggle

continuum

Continuum
The Tower Building
11 York Road
London SE1 7NX

80 Maiden Lane
Suite 704
New York, NY 10038

British Library Cataloguing-in-Publication Data
A catalogue record for this book is available from the British Library.

ISBN: 0-8264-8562-6 (hardback)
      0-8246-8563-4 (paperback)

ISBN 13: 978-08264-8562-5 (hardback)
         978-08264-8563-2 (paperback)

Library of Congress Cataloging-in-Publication Data
A catalog record for this book is available from the Library of Congress.

Typeset by Servis Filmsetting Ltd, Manchester
Printed and bound in Great Britain by MPG Books Ltd, Bodmin, Cornwall.

Contents

Introduction

What is the Renaissance? Perhaps the first thing to say is that it is not a term which anyone at the time would have used. We use the term 'Renaissance' to denote, broadly speaking, the period from *c*.1500 to *c*.1640, but the *Oxford English Dictionary* notes no instance of its use before 1840, when it appears in inverted commas as a French term, and not until the twentieth century did it become a standard description of a literary and historical period. The logic of the term is to signal the period's interest in the classical past: 'Renaissance' means 'rebirth', and what was being reborn was classical learning, lost during the Dark Ages but now recovered through the labours of scholars (initially mainly Italian) who called themselves humanists, because they were recovering knowledge which was centred on humans and their experiences.

Some modern scholars have felt that we should not necessarily stick with the term 'Renaissance', and have preferred to refer to the sixteenth and seventeenth centuries as 'the early modern period'. This is partly because 'Renaissance' describes only the experiences of the small, educated elite who were engaged with classical learning rather than the vast majority of the population, and partly to stress the idea that what we are seeing here is essentially the origins of our own period, rather than some alien and different world. However, we have preferred the term 'Renaissance', because even though the word itself was not one which people at the time would have understood, the concept certainly was: the idea of the relationship with the classical past lay at the heart of much of what the period as a whole was interested in.

Furthermore, this book is only about a small part of what other studies might refer to as the 'Renaissance'. It is focused on Britain more than Europe, on England more than Britain, on London more than the rest of England, and on English-language literature (rather than any of the many other cultural forms one might consider part of the Renaissance), and its coverage is determined by what is most relevant to illustrate and explain those works normally considered as 'Renaissance literature'.

The Renaissance period is generally reckoned as having produced some of the finest achievements of English literature, a perception centred usually on the figure of Shakespeare, who will make his way in and out of the discussions that follow. But the Renaissance period is of interest as more than just a background to Shakespeare's greatest plays. It is a period which played out crucial debates about the nature of Englishness and Britishness; the relation of Britain to Europe and the world; British politics, British language and British religion, the consequences of which can still be felt across the world today.

The guide that follows is divided into four sections. Chapter 1 provides a short historical background to the period as a whole, with illustrative examples from Renaissance literature; Chapter 2 focuses on that literature *as* literature, looking at formal and generic features; and Chapter 3 addresses 'critical approaches', the ideas which one brings to any discussion of these texts. Chapter 4 offers some starting points for independent work on the texts of this period.

1

Historical, Cultural and Intellectual Context

Politics and Economics
Religion
Science and Technology
Art and Culture
Social Structures

POLITICS AND ECONOMICS

The Reformation

It is impossible to talk about politics in the sixteenth or seventeenth centuries without also mentioning religion. This is particularly true when it comes to the Reformation, which started as an attempt to reform the Roman Catholic Church but ultimately gave rise to the very different sect of Protestantism.

Two principal causes came together to produce the English Reformation. The first was political. In 1509, the 18-year-old Henry VIII succeeded to the throne of his father Henry VII, the first king of the Tudor dynasty. The Tudors did not have a strong dynastic claim to the throne – Henry VII had won the crown in battle, killing Richard III at Bosworth in 1485 – and the turmoil of the Wars of the Roses, of which Bosworth had been the last battle, was only one generation in the past. The most urgent issue facing Henry VIII was therefore the need to marry and father children to secure his dynasty. He chose as his wife Catherine of Aragon, the widow of his elder brother, Prince Arthur. Catherine was older than Henry, but her parents, Ferdinand of Aragon and Isabella of Castile, had united Spain for the first time, and her sisters had married into the ruling families of Portugal and Burgundy (which then included the Netherlands), so, dynastically, she was a magnificent match. However, the marriage produced only one child who survived beyond babyhood, and that was a daughter, Mary. England had not had a successful queen regnant (that is, one who reigned in her own right, as opposed to being the wife of a king) since the days of the legendary Boadicea. In any case, Henry wanted a son. His dissatisfaction at Catherine's failure to produce one was compounded when he fell in love with Anne Boleyn, the daughter of an obscure Kentish knight. Henry had had mistresses before, but Anne held out for marriage.

The obvious solution seemed to be a divorce. Although divorces were impossible to obtain under normal circumstances, popes had usually been willing to annul the marriages of kings whose wives did not bear sons, and Henry could point to the fact that Catherine had been previously married to his elder brother, so the marriage could be seen as technically incestuous. However, there was a complication. Catherine's nephew, the Holy Roman Emperor Charles V, was currently holding the pope prisoner, and the pope could not offend his captor by annulling the marriage of his aunt. He dismissed Henry's request.

At any earlier period of history, that would almost certainly have been the end of the matter. The pope, who was seen as the successor of Christ's disciple St Peter, was the sole, supreme and unquestioned ruler of the entire Catholic Church (and hence the spiritual overlord of virtually everyone in Europe, apart from those few territories where Jews were still tolerated). But on 31 October 1517 a disillusioned former monk called Martin Luther had nailed 95 theses questioning the doctrines and authority of the Catholic Church to the door of the Castle Church in Wittenberg, and had effectively launched what soon became known as the Reformation. Initially designed as a process of 'reforming' or purifying the Catholic Church, this soon moved to complete opposition to Catholicism and came to be known as Protestantism. It was making many converts, including Anne Boleyn, who had been exposed to Lutheran ideas while she was finishing her education at the French court. It also provided Henry VIII with a framework of ideas with which to challenge the pope's authority and his decision not to grant him a divorce.

Although it is important to stress that Henry VIII never became a Protestant himself – indeed his view was that he himself was still a good Catholic, and that it was the pope who had deviated from the true path – he did nevertheless take the steps that launched England on the road to full-blown Protestantism. In 1533 he declared that he was the Supreme Governor of the Church of England, and appointed the Lutheran-minded Thomas Cranmer as Archbishop of Canterbury. Cranmer promptly declared that Henry's marriage to Catherine had never been valid and officiated at the wedding of Henry to the now-pregnant Anne Boleyn (though she, too, fell from favour when the child she was carrying proved to be a daughter, the future Elizabeth I). Partly because he feared that Catherine of Aragon's offended nephew, the Emperor, would make war on him, Henry also ordered the closure of all England's numerous and wealthy abbeys and monasteries, thus changing England's landscape for ever and causing a massive redistribution of wealth. He gave some of the land confiscated from the monasteries to knights and nobles, thus cementing their loyalty to him, and spent much of the money on ships (most famously the Mary Rose) intended to ward off the invasion which he feared would come from either France or Spain as a result of his decision to break with the pope, thus founding the British navy. While Henry's reign is best known for his six wives – two divorced, two beheaded (one of them Elizabeth's mother Anne Boleyn), one died and one survived – the changes that it wrought on Elizabethan society were much more profound.

Elizabeth I

Elizabeth, the baby who had been in Anne Boleyn's womb when Henry VIII married her, inherited the naval strength which her father had begun to build, but she also inherited the religious and political tensions which had made it necessary. When Henry died in 1547, he was succeeded in the first instance by the 10-year-old Edward VI, the son whom Henry's third wife, Jane Seymour, had finally given him. When Edward died in 1553, Mary Tudor, sometimes known as 'Bloody Mary' or, more properly, Mary I, who was the daughter of Henry and Catherine of Aragon, came to the throne (note that she is not the same person as Mary, Queen of Scots), but she too died in 1558. Elizabeth, the only surviving child of Henry VIII, succeeded her half-sister. Although the reign of Mary had set a precedent for the presence of a woman on the English throne, it had not been a particularly successful one: Queen Mary had had to suppress a rebellion by supporters of her cousin, Lady Jane Grey, at the start of her reign, had been bitterly disappointed not to produce a child, and had eventually died relatively young, knowing that her crown would inevitably pass to a half-sister who would reverse everything she had tried to do in the matter of religion. Parliament begged Elizabeth to marry, so that she could be 'properly' guided by a husband and could produce heirs, but there was also great disquiet about this prospect, not least because Queen Mary's husband, Philip of Spain, had been extremely unpopular in England.

However, Elizabeth did not marry. Perhaps she might have done so if her childhood friend, Robert Dudley, Earl of Leicester, had been free, but he was already married by the time she came to the throne, and when his wife died in suspicious circumstances (she was found dead at the foot of a flight of stairs), the scandal would have been too great to risk. Instead Elizabeth ruled alone, with the help of her council, headed by William Cecil, Lord Burghley. Thus, if politics in the reign of Henry VIII revolved around the king's need for a son, politics in the reign of Elizabeth centred on the queen's gender. In the early part of the reign, this also affected her relationship with neighbouring powers, as she played for as long as she could with holding out the possibility that she might marry one or other of her many foreign suitors, who included the Archduke of Austria, Philip of Spain, King Erik of Sweden, and the younger brother of the King of France. However, Elizabeth was already 25 when she came to the throne, and well before her 45-year reign drew to a close, it was abundantly apparent that her child-bearing years were over and that she would not marry.

If a queen was an anomaly in the first place, an unmarried queen – indeed an unmarried woman at all in this period – was even more of one (the legal position at the time was that all women, of whatever age, were considered to be either married or about to be married). Elizabeth benefited, however, from an unforeseen effect of the Reformation. The disappearance of the intercessory role of the Virgin Mary and of the saints, many of whom were female, had left a psychological and cultural gap which a virgin queen was exceptionally well placed to fill. As a result, something of a cult developed around the queen, with a number of mythological personae, most notably various versions of the moon goddess, used to represent her, and these became a crucial part of the queen's public image.

An unusual coincidence meant that the question of the queen's image was particularly important, because the British Isles, which had known no reigning queen for many hundreds of years, now suddenly had two. In neighbouring Scotland, then an entirely separate and independent country from England, Henry VIII's nephew, King James V, had died young and been succeeded by his only surviving child, a week-old daughter called Mary (not to be confused with Elizabeth's elder half-sister Mary Tudor). While still only a child, the little queen had been sent to France and married to the eldest son of the French king, but her husband died shortly after succeeding to the crown and Mary returned to Scotland as a young widow, speaking only French, a Catholic in a Protestant country, and thoroughly alienated from her homeland and subjects. She made a disastrous marriage to her cousin, Henry, Lord Darnley, and though this marriage gave her a son, the future James VI, it ended soon afterwards with the mysterious murder of Darnley. When Mary immediately married the chief suspect, James Hepburn, Earl of Bothwell, the Scots, already shocked by her Catholicism and what was seen as her frivolous behaviour, rebelled. Mary was imprisoned, but escaped to England, presenting Elizabeth with a serious problem. As a Protestant, Elizabeth had no desire to offend her Protestant Scottish neighbours, who were currently causing her no trouble; but as a queen herself, she wanted to show the importance of respecting the rights of other queens.

The compromise she arrived at was to imprison Mary in England, an imprisonment which ultimately lasted for 19 years. This led to badly strained relations with France, of which Mary had once, however briefly, been queen consort, and with Spain, where Philip II, already outraged by Henry VIII's treatment of his great-aunt, Catherine of Aragon, was now appalled by England's imprisonment of another Catholic queen. (Philip was further irritated by Elizabeth's toleration of English privateers intercepting Spanish ships, something which will be discussed below under Concepts of Value.) As a result, an atmosphere of extreme paranoia about domestic security developed in England. Catholics became increasingly suspect and, under Sir Francis Walsingham, the English government developed its first intelligence service, for which Christopher Marlowe and Edmund Spenser, among others, appear to have worked. There was a feverish atmosphere of plots and counterplots, culminating in the execution of Mary, Queen of Scots in 1587 after Walsingham's spies had secured evidence of her willingness to be involved in a plot to assassinate Elizabeth.

The execution of Mary brought hostilities with Spain to a head. Philip had prepared an 'Invincible Armada' of ships to sail against England, to bring it back into the Catholic fold. The armada would have sailed as soon as the news of Mary's death reached Madrid, but the weather prevented it. The

English anxiously awaited invasion throughout 1587 (the year of Christopher Marlowe's *Tamburlaine*) and the first half of 1588, until the Invincible Armada finally sailed in the summer of 1588 – and was dispersed by storms, which the English interpreted as 'God's Wind'.

Elizabeth's troubles were by no means over, however. Although Philip's plans to invade England had suffered a setback from which they would never recover, he was still active elsewhere in Europe. A series of early deaths and dynastic failures had given Philip's father, the Emperor Charles V, an extraordinary collection of territories. Charles's mother, Juana the Mad (the sister of Catherine of Aragon), had inherited both the Spanish crown and the Spanish territories of the New World; his father, Philip the Fair, was the heir to Burgundy, which included what are now the Low Countries or Netherlands. Travel between these many dominions was difficult if not impossible, and first Charles and then Philip ruled the Low Countries through a series of regents. Inevitably, it proved difficult to retain their hold on the territory, especially after Protestantism began to spread through the Netherlands. Philip repressed this with increasing ferocity, sending the brutal Duke of Alva to suppress the rebellion against Spanish rule. The Dutch appealed to Elizabeth, as a fellow Protestant, and she responded by sending her close friend (some said lover), the Earl of Leicester, at the head of a military expedition to support the rebels. With Leicester went his nephew and heir, Sir Philip Sidney, author of the sonnet sequence *Astrophil and Stella* and of *The Countess of Pembroke's Arcadia*, who was to meet his death there. The English military presence in the Netherlands gave the Low Countries a high profile in English politics for the remainder of the queen's reign.

The final arena of Elizabethan military activity was Ireland. Because this was largely Catholic, the English government feared that it could be used as a back door for a Spanish invasion. Although normally parsimonious, Elizabeth spent a great deal of money on trying to subdue native Irish resistance, but successive English armies were defeated by the terrain and the Irish fighters' superior local knowledge. Finally, Elizabeth sent her last favourite, Robert Devereux, Earl of Essex, son of her cousin and stepson of Leicester, to Ireland. Essex saw himself as a military hero, but he too was unable to reduce the Irish to submission. Desperate to explain his failure to do so, he returned to England without permission. Legend has it that he arrived so early in the morning that he caught the queen without her wig and make-up on; he certainly plunged so far from favour that in 1601 he decided that his one remaining option was to lead the only armed rebellion of Elizabeth's reign. It was a miserable failure. Essex was executed and the queen lived out the last years of her reign in peace, dying in 1603, certainly less popular than she had been, but still undisputed Queen of England.

James and Charles

Elizabeth's successor was James VI of Scotland, the only child of Mary, Queen of Scots. James, who had been King of Scotland since he was a baby, was now in his late thirties, married to a Danish princess, and the father of several children. On all these grounds he seemed at first a welcome change from Elizabeth, but his initial popularity soon cooled. James had two major political projects: he wanted to bring an end to all hostilities with foreign powers, and he wanted to unite his separate inheritances of Scotland, England, Wales and Ireland into a 'British Empire'. Peace in Ireland came courtesy of a victory by Essex's brother-in-law, Lord Mountjoy, which actually occurred during the last days of Elizabeth's reign, but which was not known in London until after her death; a much less popular move came when James also made a peace treaty with Spain.

James's domestic life was less peaceful than his foreign policy. Almost certainly homosexual, he was even more susceptible to male favourites than Elizabeth had been, and not always wise in those he selected. This gave rise to a number of scandals at his court, of which the most notable centred on the murder of Sir Thomas Overbury on the orders of

Frances Howard, who sought a divorce from her first husband, Robert, Earl of Essex (the son of Elizabeth's favourite), so she could marry Robert Carr, Earl of Somerset (King James's favourite). Overbury, who was Carr's friend, advised him against the marriage, and promptly found himself imprisoned in the Tower of London, where he died. At the divorce hearing, Frances claimed to be a virgin, and a masked woman who may or may not have been her was physically examined behind a screen to 'prove' this. This caused a scandal which is echoed in a number of Jacobean plays, including Middleton and Rowley's *The Changeling*. It is little wonder that the corruption of princes' courts is a recurrent theme of the tragedy of the period.

James lived a life which was largely separate from that of his queen, Anne of Denmark, who had secretly converted to Catholicism (before his accession, James had promised toleration for Catholics, but this had not materialized). Neither was he close to his eldest son, Prince Henry. Possibly James was jealous, for Henry and his sister Elizabeth were wildly popular and regarded as offering hope for the future. But Henry died of typhoid in 1612, and it was James's youngest surviving child, Charles, who eventually succeeded him in 1625 as Charles I. A sickly and unpromising child, Charles grew into an obstinate and remote king, emotionally dependent first on his father's great favourite, the Duke of Buckingham, and then, after Buckingham's assassination in 1628, on his French queen Henrietta Maria, who was very unpopular because of her very public Catholicism. Charles's increasingly strained relationship with Parliament led to its suspension in 1629, after which the theatre took on something of the role of Parliament, in being one of the few places where political questions could be openly discussed. In 1642, war broke out between the king and Parliament, resulting in the immediate closing of the theatres, and effectively marking the end of the Renaissance period. After seven years of hostilities, Charles was beheaded in 1649 on the orders of Parliament, and from then on until 1660, England was not under the control of a king.

Economics: concepts of value

This was a period of rapidly increasing international trade. The discovery of America in 1492 opened up the immensely valuable trade in silver from the New World, initially monopolized by Spain but subject to increasingly successful attacks by English privateers such as Sir Francis Drake. On the other side of the world, the fabulous riches offered by the Spice Islands of Indonesia led to increasingly frantic efforts to locate either a north-west or a north-east passage, which would offer a short cut to them. In between, the Muscovy Company, initially under the direction of Sir Philip Sidney's father, Henry, was attempting to open up the markets of Russia, which it saw as lucrative not only in its own right but also as the gateway to Asia. All this led to a radical shift in what was considered profitable; 'commodities', or tradeable objects, were considered more exciting than land, not least because there seemed no limit to what they might potentially be worth. When the Chorus in *Henry V* observes that 'they sell the pasture now to buy the horse', he might well be seen as hitting the nail on the head in identifying a growing trend to value consumables over land. At the same time, a series of bad harvests began in the 1590s, growing steadily worse and culminating in food riots in the Midlands in 1608, of which echoes can be heard in both *A Midsummer Night's Dream* and *Coriolanus*. However, Elizabeth devoted considerable effort to standardizing weights, measures and distances, and was so proud of her achievement in stabilizing the currency that it is mentioned on her tomb.

RELIGION

The population of Renaissance England was, by modern standards, fervently religious. 'Atheist' was an insult too extreme and too ludicrous to be taken literally. Specifically, everyone was Christian: that is, they believed that God's own son Jesus had taken human form in order to be killed, and so take on himself the punishment for the sins which humanity had committed, enabling humanity to be forgiven for them. Beyond that, the disagreements began. In John Webster's play *The White Devil*, a ghost returns to earth. The man who sees it immediately demands, 'Pray, sir, resolve me, what religion's best / For a man to die in?' (5.4.131–2). There were few more important questions in Renaissance England, and few which were more difficult to answer. Two of the religions which are to be discussed here, Judaism and Islam, were widely demonized in Renaissance England; however, that still left a difficult and agonizing choice between the various branches (the technical term is 'confessions') into which Christianity had split in the wake of the Reformation. Matters were not made easier by the fact that there were two entirely separate influences at work on the choice of confession, and that these often pulled in entirely different directions. In the first place, there was personal preference, whether in the form of a deeply held theological or spiritual conviction, or of family tradition or pressure – Elizabethan Catholics, in particular, tended to transmit their views very strongly to their children. In the second, however, there was government policy, which was inevitably influenced to some extent, though not wholly directed, by the personal preferences of the monarch. Thus England was officially still Catholic under Henry VIII, despite the king's quarrel with the pope, because Henry took the imperious view that he still maintained the true traditions of the Catholic Church and that it was the pope who had moved away from them. The country became Protestant under his son Edward VI (1547–53); it reverted to Catholicism again under Mary I (1553–8); and it became broadly Protestant under Elizabeth I (1558–1603), who, despite her personal wish to find a middle way and not 'make windows into men's souls' – that is, to allow people to follow the dictates of their conscience in private as long as they conformed in public – was forced to clamp down on Catholicism after Pope Pius excommunicated her in 1570 and thus effectively gave Catholics a licence to kill her.

Catholicism

Christianity had been the dominant religion in England since St Augustine, the apostle of England, arrived in Kent in 597 AD. (He initiated Canterbury Cathedral, in the shadow of which Christopher Marlowe grew up.) By the time Henry VIII came to the throne in 1509, Christianity was entirely synonymous with Catholicism; by the time he died in 1547, it had split into the two very different confessions, Catholicism and Protestantism. Although Henry continued to define himself as Catholic, Catholicism was effectively an endangered religion from 1533 onwards, and except for a brief interlude during the reign of Mary Tudor (1553–8), individual Catholics were likely to be persecuted and in many cases even martyred. Despite this, many people continued to adhere to Catholicism in varyingly public ways, and very few people, except perhaps radical Puritans, abandoned entirely all the beliefs and practices associated with the Old Religion, as it was sometimes called.

The two principal doctrinal differences between Protestantism and Catholicism centred on the relationship between man and God, and the fate of the soul after death. For Catholics, the priest was an essential mediator between the word of God and the lay (i.e. non-clerical) person. Both the translation of the Bible from Latin and private study of the Bible were discouraged: the word of God was what the priest said it was. Protestants, by contrast, encouraged personal reading of the Bible and stressed the idea of individual communication with God: in a sense, every man or woman became his or her own priest (though women, belonging as they did to the weaker sex, were generally understood to require the help of their husbands in this). This emphasis on personal interaction with the Word was undoubtedly a major stimulus to the spread of literacy and the growth of print culture during the Renaissance, but it could also seem alarming, in that it placed far more responsibility on the individual. This was even more the case because Protestantism downplayed the importance of the saints and particularly of the Virgin Mary, who could thus no longer be appealed to as intercessors, compassionate mediating figures who could appeal to God on behalf of sinful humans. All across Protestant Europe, statues and images of the saints were destroyed in a wave of iconoclasm (image-breaking).

The other major difference concerned belief in purgatory. Catholics believed that unless an individual died in a state of grace, the soul would enter a kind of halfway house between heaven and hell. Although purgatory was a painful place, all was not lost because it was possible to say prayers and masses for deceased loved ones and to light candles for the benefit of their souls, and thus eventually to help them progress to heaven. There was thus a kind of second chance for people even after they are dead. Protestants, however, believed only in heaven and in hell. You were either saved or you were damned, and there were no second chances. This is an even more alarming idea than the need for individual communication with God, and there is clear evidence that the saying of prayers for the dead was something that lingered a long time in Renaissance England, particularly in rural areas and regions distant from London (Catholicism was particularly persistent in the north, where many of the major rebellions against Protestant governments originated). Saying prayers for the dead gave people comfort and they clung to the practice long after the Church of England had entirely disavowed it. The continued belief in the possibility of interaction with the dead may also help us to understand some of what is going on in *Hamlet*, when the prince, who will doubtless have received an impeccably Protestant education at Wittenberg, home of Martin Luther, finds himself face to face with the ghost of his father, something which would be an impossibility in Protestant theology.

As well as these two major areas of disagreement between the two confessions, there were also other differences. There were, for instance, different views on the question of marriage and celibacy. Celibacy had been an important idea in Catholic medieval England, and large communities of monks and nuns had been a prominent feature of life. Henry VIII changed all that for ever by ordering the Dissolution of the Monasteries. Protestants did not value celibacy for its own sake and, though virginity before marriage continued to remain important, this was for social rather than religious reasons. In Protestant eyes matrimony was important both as a concept and as a fundamental part of a well-ordered society, and it was perfectly acceptable for widows to remarry, something which Catholics were much more likely to frown on. Catholics also observed a cycle of feast and fast, feasting on saints' days and adhering strictly to the policy of eating only fish rather than meat on Fridays and other designated days of penance, and practised various other forms of ritual behaviour.

Protestantism

Although it is convenient to refer to the rise of Protestantism in the sixteenth century, it is really something of a misnomer, because the term 'Protestant' covers a number of different theological positions. When Martin Luther nailed his 95 theses to the door of the Castle Church in Wittenberg on 31 October 1517 and set in train the Reformation, his followers were initially known primarily as Lutherans. Luther, however, was by no means the only Protestant theologian directing the course of the new ideas. Particularly influential was John Calvin (1509–64), an exiled French Protestant living in Geneva. Calvin's major contribution to the current of Protestant thought was to formulate the concept of pre-destination. Essentially, he declared that all human beings are either elect – destined for heaven – or damned, and that this has already been predestined by God *before the individual has even been born*. Thus it is theoretically possible for a person to lead an entirely blameless life and yet nevertheless be destined for hell, or alternatively to commit sins and yet nevertheless be among the elect. The principal difference between the damned and the elect while on earth is that God allows the elect the grace to repent of any sins they may commit, while the damned are unable to do so. This concept is interestingly illustrated by a small but highly suggestive variant in the two different texts of Christopher Marlowe's play *Doctor Faustus*. (It is difficult to be sure which to prefer because both of these very different texts of the play appeared well after Marlowe's death in 1593, and both contain references to events which postdate his lifetime, and so must have been added by someone else.) In the 1616 B text, the Good Angel tells Faustus that it is 'Never too late, if Faustus will repent'. This would be the standard Lutheran position: repentance is possible if the person chooses it. In the 1604 A text, however, the Good Angel's words are 'Never too late, if Faustus can repent'. To Renaissance ears, this is a very different concept: 'can repent' indicates the Calvinist position that it may be impossible to repent because God may have chosen to withhold from the individual the grace that would enable him or her to do so. Claudius in *Hamlet* also finds that he cannot repent, even though he wants to. This idea that humans may have no choice in the matter, that their spiritual fate may already have been decided and that nothing whatsoever that they can do can influence it, is an extremely alarming one for people who seriously believe in the possibility of eternal damnation, and helps explain why so many people clung to the much more forgiving approach of Catholicism, with its second chance in purgatory and its intercessory saints.

Puritanism

Calvinism was by no means the only alternative form that Protestantism might take. As the period progressed, Puritanism becomes an ever more important force. To some extent 'Puritan' is just a catch-all insult: Maria in *Twelfth Night*, for instance, calls Malvolio 'a kind of Puritan', though there is no evidence whatever about his religious beliefs; and although Sir Andrew Aguecheek immediately declares that if he thought Malvolio was a Puritan he would beat him like a dog, Sir Toby Belch does not seem to share his friend's assumptions here, asking 'What, for being a Puritan? Thy exquisite reason, dear knight?' (2.3.125–8). Essentially, Puritans are self-identified as those who wish to be, or believe that they are, 'purer' in their religious observances than their fellow Protestants. They are likely to shun all forms of ceremony or observance, disliking the use of music, incense or genuflection (kneeling) in religious services, not celebrating Christmas with any form of secular festivity, and in some cases not even allowing wedding rings, since these are unnecessary physical manifestations of a union existing on the spiritual plane. Because the Church of England dismissed them as extremists, Puritans are also oppositional figures, who were ultimately to play a central part in the growing challenge to Stuart rule which eventually led to the dethroning and execution of Charles I in 1649. In the earlier Renaissance period, however, the principal manifestation of the move towards Puritanism was the Martin Marprelate tracts, a pamphlet war of 1588–90 in which various literary figures such as Thomas Nashe were involved, and of which echoes are sometimes heard in the literature of the period. The comic name of the fictitious pamphleteer, Martin Marprelate, indicates another main tenet of Puritan ideology: distrust of 'prelates', bishops and clergy in general. But this is a political as well as a religous activism, since a rejection of the authority of bishops opens the way for a Puritan to start to doubt the authority of the king who is their head.

Judaism and Islam

Widespread fears and misconceptions about both Judaism and Islam operated in Renaissance England to make Muslims (particularly Turks) and Jews stock villains in Renaissance drama. In the case of Islam, a general intolerance of all religions other than Christianity was backed up by the fact that the Turks really were a growing world power who were felt to pose a terrible threat to Christian Europe. Since the fall of Constantinople in 1453, Turkish power had been creeping ever nearer; Vienna had been besieged, and in 1565 Turkey had only narrowly failed to capture the

Mediterranean island of Malta, something which is recalled in Christopher Marlowe's play *The Jew of Malta*. Christian victories, such as the survival of Malta and the Venetians' defeat of the Turks at the Battle of Lepanto in 1571, were celebrated all over Europe, providing some of the few occasions on which otherwise warring Catholics and Protestants could rejoice together at the defeat of a common enemy. In the case of Judaism, there was no comparable political power to generate a real or perceived threat to European security, but that did not stop the most rabid of myths circulating about the Jews and their supposed wickedness and malice.

This widespread demonization of both Judaism and Islam gives rise to a number of stereotypes which are repeatedly drawn on in English Renaissance drama. Muslim characters in Renaissance plays are often the butt of jokes about eunuchs, derived from the fact that the harems of Turkish sultans were indeed guarded only by eunuchs. They are often represented as sexually interested in white women, and this is something that we might well want to remember in connection with Shakespeare's *Othello*, where 'the Moor' may be clearly understood as a convert from Islam. Othello's epilepsy may also be due to the fact that Mohammed was frequently (though falsely) said in the Renaissance to have been an epileptic: the Islamic religion was understood as essentially the product of a hallucinatory vision that he experienced during a fit. Certainly few tears were likely to be shed over the death of a Muslim character in a Renaissance play, and Turks in particular become a byword for lust, cruelty and untrustworthiness. They are portrayed on stage in a number of plays of the period, such as John Mason's *The Turk*, and the fighting at the edges of the Turkish empire is a presence in plays including Shakespeare's *Othello* and Marlowe's *The Jew of Malta*.

The Jew of Malta also provides one of the two most memorable stage Jews of the period, in its central character Barabas, who can be compared with Shylock in Shakespeare's *The Merchant of Venice*, a figure clearly influenced by Marlowe's portrayal of Barabas. The Jews were persecuted throughout Europe, and had been expelled from England as early as 1290. Although there were a very few Jews remaining in Elizabethan England, they had to keep a very low profile and were liable to persecution, as when the Jewish Dr Lopez was executed in 1594 on almost certainly trumped-up charges of plotting to poison Queen Elizabeth. Very few people in England, therefore, had actually met a Jew, but that did not stop them from confidently entertaining a number of preconceptions about them, the most unlikely of which was the widely held belief that Jewish men menstruated. Other stereotypical characteristics of the Jew in the period were avarice and usury, abundantly demonstrated in both Barabas and Shylock. Above all, though, Jews were vilified because they were held responsible for the death of Christ, something which is recalled in the fact that Marlowe ironically gives his Jew the name of Barabas, who in the biblical story is the convicted criminal whom the Jews select in preference to Christ when Pilate offers, according to custom, to release one prisoner. They were also often slurred with the 'blood libel', the allegation that Jews abducted and killed Christian children.

Witchcraft and magic

There is one more belief system which needs to be mentioned, even though it was quite different from the others. This is witchcraft, which was widely believed in during the Renaissance. 'Witch crazes' swept through Germany and also to a lesser extent through Scotland, where King James VI (later also King James I of England) became convinced of the existence of witches after an old woman apparently recounted to him with complete accuracy what he had said to his bride on their wedding night. As a result, he published a treatise called *Daemonologie* in Edinburgh in 1597, and in 1603, when he came south to take the throne of England, it was printed in London, too. A number of women were executed for witchcraft in England during the Renaissance, and many plays reflect the public interest in the subject, from Shakespeare's *Macbeth* to more factually based works such as Dekker, Ford and Rowley's *The Witch of Edmonton* and Heywood and Brome's *The Late Lancashire Witches*, both based on actual witch trials.

The possibility of magic was also taken seriously. The self-styled magus John Dee was consulted by Queen Elizabeth about the most auspicious date for her coronation, and summoned to Prague to converse with the Emperor Rudolf. Magic was not necessarily understood as antithetical to religion – popes consulted astrologers – and it was thought seriously possible that it might open the door to a variety of secrets, not least the philosopher's stone, which was supposed to turn base metal into gold and enable its possessor to enjoy eternal life. Dee, who believed that his sidekick, Edward Kelley, conversed with angels (though the main message of the 'angels' was that Kelley should be allowed to sleep with Mrs Dee), was an influential figure in Elizabethan England, coining the phrase 'the British Empire' and serving as a possible model for both Marlowe's Doctor Faustus and Shakespeare's Prospero.

SCIENCE AND TECHNOLOGY

As the credence accorded to Kelley's angels shows, throughout the Renaissance period Britain was and remained, by today's standards, primitive in its science and technology. On the other hand, Renaissance British writers frequently express the view that they are living in a period of white-hot technological and scientific revolution. This paradox invites further consideration of what exactly Renaissance science and technology were. The challenge of Renaissance literature is to imagine, not merely life without electricity or petrochemicals, but a whole pre-industrial culture in which print is a luxury technology; even local travel is difficult and limited; and scientists and magicians are the same people.

Science

A favourite Renaissance idea is that each individual person is a 'microcosm' – a little world in his or her own right – and that this little world reflects and is in tune with the 'macrocosm' – the universe on its largest scale. Neither the Renaissance's microcosm nor its macrocosm much resembles its modern equivalent.

On the microcosmic level, it was taken for granted that everyone had a soul, and that the body was merely a temporary and probably inherently sinful container for it. Indeed, some poems of the period – Donne's 'The Ecstasy' or Marvell's 'A Dialogue Between the Soul and Body' – develop this idea, figuring the body almost as a giant robot, within which the soul sits like a human pilot. In a society where the basic principles of hygiene were unknown, it was also taken for granted that many children would die at birth or soon thereafter, while adults, too, were used to living with the possibility that they might suddenly die from disease. In addition, in some summers outbreaks of the plague swept through London, closing the theatres and prompting the wealthy to escape into the countryside until the plague had died down. In such a world, the death of the body was not an unspeakable secret, but an everyday reality.

The governing principle of medical theory was the idea that human bodies – like everything else in the universe – were made up of varying proportions of the four elements: earth (cold and dry), water (cold and wet), air (warm and wet) and fire (warm and dry). In people, these elements were manifested most directly as the four 'humours' of the body, the fluids – respectively black bile, phlegm, blood and yellow bile – which were believed to derive from the four elements. Every individual had slightly different amounts of these four humours, which, when mixed together, created their personality: hence, a person with an unusually high proportion of blood would be 'sanguine', given to high spirits and optimism. Hence, too, people might be displaying personalities that were predominantly 'choleric' –

short-tempered, from an excess of yellow bile – or 'phleg-matic' – patient, from an excess of phlegm. Hamlet, with his habitual misery, air of mystery and penchant for wearing black, is seen by Polonius as a classic case of the 'melancholy' personality: his eccentric behaviour, thinks Polonius, is caused not by existential doubts but by an excess of black bile inside his body.

The balance of humours in one's body could be affected by environmental factors, particularly by diet, and illness was what happened when the balance was disturbed. The goal of most early modern medical treatment, therefore, was to restore the supposed balance of the humours, by expelling the excess: this could involve strong laxatives, or alternatively bleeding by cutting open a vein or by applying leeches. In the circumstances, it is remarkable that the patients continued to believe (as they did) that this was doing them good.

Another aspect of medical theory worth mention is the one-sex model, also known as the Galenic theory of sex. Many early modern theorists tended to believe that men and women were fundamentally different: in terms of the balance of elements in their bodies, even in terms of their biological origin, since, according to the Bible, woman was created after man, out of man, and is therefore an inferior copy. But the one-sex model puts the emphasis differently, arguing that men and women have the same bodies, but merely arranged differently: the structure of the genitals could fold inwards to make you a woman, or outwards to make you a man. Indeed, in one famous case, a French girl's genitals were alleged to have sprung outwards when she jumped over a ditch, quickly turning her into a man. Not everyone believed such stories, but the fact that the model was available to think with, the idea that gender might not be entirely biologically stable, is an interesting one to bring to the cross-dressing heroines of Shakespeare's *Twelfth Night* or *As You Like It*.

Undeterred by their uncertainties about the nature of the body, and the fact that their main treatments were worse than useless, doctors studied the elaborate theory of their science, mapping the four humours on to the 12 astrological signs, and in many cases using astrological charts in their treatment planning. While this seems bizarre today, it reflects a Renaissance world-view in which everything is holistic, connected to everything else in mysterious ways which a truly wise man might be able to perceive. Another favourite image for exploring this idea is the 'great chain of being' – the idea that everything in the universe is connected, in order of perfection, with God at the top of the chain. The twentieth-century critic E. M. W. Tillyard argued that such accounts gave rise to the 'Elizabethan world-picture', an imagined mindset in which there was great and instinctive respect for hierarchy and degree in all its forms: but, as later critics have noted, it is hard entirely to reconcile this idea with early modern literature, in which forms of degree and order are often questioned, mocked, or even turned completely upside down.

Early modern macrocosmic thinking is seen in its most extreme form in the theory of spheres, also referred to as the Ptolemaic model of the universe. In this model, the earth is round – indeed, the earth has always been thought of as round: the idea that medieval Europe believed in a flat earth is a twentieth-century myth. This round ball is encased in a giant, transparent glassy sphere, which contains the moon, and which rotates swiftly around the earth. Around this, arranged like a set of Russian dolls, are other, ever larger spheres, containing the other planets, the sun and the stars. As the spheres move around each other, they create a heavenly sound (the 'music of the spheres'). Strange as this theory may seem, it provided the basis for accurate astronomical predictions; and while its validity was increasingly doubted, especially after Nicolaus Copernicus proposed that the earth might travel around the sun rather than vice versa, it took the observations of Galileo in the 1610s, dependent upon the invention of the telescope, to start to thoroughly dismantle the Ptolemaic system. Nonetheless, it lives on in the poetry of Donne, Milton and many others.

Linked to the theory of spheres was that of alchemy, since alchemy posited magical relationships between individual spheres and individual metals. Alchemy combined what would now be categorized as chemical and physical science with what would now be categorized as magic, in an era when the distinction between the two had not yet been established. Alchemists, including the famous John Dee mentioned in the previous section, were equally at home distilling chemicals and conversing with spirits, worked both with the material world and with demons, and their ultimate aim was to discover the philosopher's stone – the substance which would transform everything around it from base metal into pure gold, the most perfect form of matter. Such a discovery would deliver massive financial power to whoever was lucky enough to own it, and many monarchs in Renaissance Europe invested heavily in alchemists in the hope of achieving such a breakthrough.

There was, however, a catch, because alchemical theory held that what is found depends on who is looking for it. In an idea familiar today from fictions about the quest for the Holy Grail, alchemists believed that only the pure of heart would be able to find the philosopher's stone. In order successfully to transform base metal into gold, the alchemist had first to transform himself into a man so entirely wise that he would no longer have any use for or interest in the resulting riches. Thus, in Ben Jonson's *The Alchemist*, the supposed alchemists use this idea of 'willing poverty' to explain why, despite the fabulous riches that they claim to be able to deliver to those they are duping, they themselves are patently very poor. The point about alchemy is that it is always both a financial venture carrying the possibility of enormous wealth, and yet also a personal, spiritual quest for the alchemist himself, as he attempts to improve his own soul and gain spiritual enlightenment. In alchemy, then, the microcosm and the macrocosm were intimately connected.

Travel

As for travel, it was slow, arduous and expensive even within Britain. Lacking tarmac, roads were muddy tracks, frequently impassable in winter. In any case, most of the large industrial cities of modern Britain hardly existed, and outside London, the largest town in England was Norwich, the centre of an important cloth trade. In the absence of powered vehicles, the best way to travel was by river, in a coach, or on a horse: horses thus occupied something of the mental space now given to cars and motorbikes, with mastery of one's horse – as in Sidney's *Astrophil and Stella*, Sonnet 49 – a powerful sign of manliness. Wealthy women rode side-saddle or in coaches.

Overseas travel was the preserve of the very wealthy, especially since it required government permission, so that Shakespeare (for instance) is not known ever to have left England, in spite of all the plays that use overseas settings. Europe was moderately well known, with established stage caricatures of other nations including the Italians (wicked, scheming poisoners with a tendency towards jealousy) and the French (untrustworthy and frivolous). Further afield, early modern Britain was aware of, and experienced uneasy trading relations with, powerful empires in the east: notably with the Sultan of the Ottoman Empire, with Ivan the Terrible and his successors as Grand Tsar of Russia, and even with the Moghul Emperor of India. Africa was much less well known, and Australia remained entirely undiscovered throughout this period.

The most exciting development in geography was the New World of North and South America, formally 'discovered' by Columbus in 1492. It represented both a spiritual threat – since it was not mentioned in the Bible, which thus appeared to be incomplete – and a spiritual opportunity, being filled with new races who clearly needed to be quickly converted to Christianity. Early modern Britain saw the Indians of the New World both as 'noble savages', innocents uncorrupted by the taint of decadent civilization, and simply as savages who needed and deserved the harshest of treatments. Caliban, in Shakespeare's *The Tempest*, a play based partly on early accounts of Bermuda, embodies both tendencies at once.

The idea of the New World was a potent blank canvas for the Renaissance imagination, ranging from Thomas More's imaginary *Utopia* to John Donne's description, in 'To his Mistress going to bed', of his mistress' naked body as 'My America, my new-found land' (Donne, 1961, 54). The reality was more prosaic. In places like Virginia (named after Queen Elizabeth I) along the eastern seaboard of North America, those colonists who had survived the voyage there struggled against starvation and disease to gain a foothold on the new continent, a battle which sometimes they lost, as in the settlement sponsored by Sir Walter Ralegh at Roanoke, which simply disappeared. Much of the serious money to be made out of the New World came from campaigns of organized piracy against the more lucrative Spanish colonies of South America. Renaissance imports from the New World included tobacco and syphilis: exports to the New World included firearms, smallpox and, as the seventeenth century wore on, religious dissenters.

Printing

Printing was the early modern equivalent of the Internet: a new method of communication that had far-reaching social consequences as people thought up new ways to use it. Of course, books could be reproduced even before the advent of printing, simply by employing a scribe with a pen to write out, longhand, a copy of an existing book. Such a process was error-prone, time-consuming and, therefore, expensive – very expensive, if the book was of any length, such as the Bible. Another option was woodblock printing, a technology developed in China and in the West. In essence, woodblock printing involves taking a flat piece of wood, and cutting away with a chisel those areas where one doesn't want ink to appear, before applying ink to the finished block and impressing it onto paper: it is the same principle as is used in potato printing. However, it too is time-consuming, and only a limited number of copies can be produced in one run, because the block wears away quickly. For these reasons, woodblock printing remained a relatively expensive medium. In the 1430s, Johannes Gutenberg, a jeweller in Mainz, developed a system of moveable type, in which a page of text, instead of being hand-carved into a single piece of wood, was assembled from dozens of small cast-metal pieces, each one bearing the raised shape of a single letter of the alphabet. The metal was a harder material, so that the print runs could be much higher; and each letter could be reused many times, so that, having printed many copies of one page, you could disassemble the type and put it back together in a different combination to print an entirely different page. In 1455, Gutenberg printed the first major book using this new system: the Bible, in Latin.

Gutenberg's discovery changed many aspects of Renaissance knowledge by making it easier, faster and cheaper to disseminate texts of all sorts. It created, slowly, an entire industry of printers, partially replacing the earlier industry of professional scribes and copyists. And there were also religious implications, because, as noted above, one of the major ideas of Protestant thinking was that the Bible itself should be read, directly, by as many people as possible. This idea was only made financially feasible by the printing technology developed by Gutenberg. Hence, the printing press was not merely a new efficient way of communication, but also an agent of change in a religious context.

On the other hand, early modern England was still, by today's standards, very limited in its access to print. All printers had to be licensed, and the only printing presses permitted in England during Elizabeth's reign were in Oxford, Cambridge and London. The Stationers' Company, a trade guild who had a lucrative monopoly on printing rights, were careful to ensure that their members published nothing seditious which might threaten that monopoly. While the volume of printing increased fast, year by year, the licensing system continued to cope with the strain until almost the outbreak of the Civil War, when the system failed and there was an explosion of unlicensed printing. Every work we read which was first printed before then has, in a sense, passed through a process of censorship.

This is not true, however, of manuscript transmission, which continued to thrive despite the advent of print. Writers of short lyric poems, in particular, would distribute them around a circle of friends for hand-copying, much as people today make copies of CDs: the process of copying was part of the social glue which held such circles together, and access to the manuscript material was an indication of one's membership of the circle. One particularly interesting example is Francis Meres' comment in a book printed in 1598 that Shakespeare has been distributing 'sugared sonnets among his private friends', something which Meres mentions casually as if to indicate that he, too, is among this in-crowd. Shakespeare's sonnets were not, however, printed until 1609. For at least those 11 years, if you were reading Shakespeare's sonnets, it was in manuscript: and it was an indication that you knew someone who knew someone who knew Shakespeare.

Manuscript transmission is different to print in another important way: unlike a mechanical reproduction, manuscript copies are never quite the same as the originals from which they are taken. In each copying, they can be expanded, updated and altered to suit the interests and beliefs of the copyist. While many manuscript variants are recognizably mistakes of transcription, others are creative acts in their own right. A famous instance, early in the period, indicates the type of problem that comes up. Sir Thomas Wyatt's lyric 'They flee from me that sometime did me seek' is a haunting poem about a relationship that has ended. The poem survives in two main variants, one recorded in a book printed in 1557 (*Tottel's Miscellany*), and one which survives in an early manuscript. The versions differ in many minor but important respects: for instance, in the penultimate line, the speaker states that the woman has served him 'kindly' in the manuscript version, and 'unkindly' in the print version (see Ferguson, 1996, 115). Later anthologies print sometimes one, sometimes the other version. A simple approach would be to ask which version is 'right', and which one is merely a copy which has made mistakes of copying; but since Wyatt's own manuscript of the poem does not survive, it is not possible to answer this question. After all, even the print version (printed 15 years after Wyatt's death) only really records whatever copied manuscript was available to that particular printer, so that it can't be said to encapsulate Wyatt's final intentions for the poem. Often, where two texts diverge like this, one or other of the readings can be identified as a mistake: but that does not apply here. Both readings make sense – indeed, part of the force of the poem lies precisely in the fact that it explores the thin line between kindness and cruelty. Whoever changed 'unkindly' to 'kindly', or vice versa, in the course of copying, intervened in a creative way in the poem. Just because it is unclear which reading came first should not prevent us from enjoying both versions.

Scholars used to believe that there was a 'stigma of print' in early modern Britain: that there was considered to be something inherently vulgar about printing one's literary works which deterred aristocrats from doing so (see May, 1980). There are, however, many exceptions to this supposed rule. It is more interesting to think in terms of the opportunities of manuscript transmission, and the ways in which print and manuscript intertwine in the period. Not just printed books, but also manuscript transmission, represent the Renaissance's advanced and powerful forms of information technology.

ART AND CULTURE

What we study as Renaissance literature tends to have been written by the elite: mostly well-educated, mostly based in London, almost all men and almost all amateurs who did not need to earn a wage for a living. There are, of course, exceptions to all four of these rules, with the playwrights Shakespeare and Jonson the most obvious exceptions to the last of them. Nonetheless, there is a natural tendency towards looking at 'high culture': art, often London-based, appealing to a privileged audience – and that is what we shall consider here. For those who wrote what we now study as literature, three particularly interesting areas of culture were the visual arts and architecture, the professional stage; and courtly performance. But before considering them, let us enumerate some of the other most prominent aspects of Renaissance culture:

- Religious culture – the weekly sermons at which attendance was compulsory, the frequent printings of those sermons, the religious tracts and psalm translations – was of central importance.
- Popular culture included the broadside ballads sold, and sung, by travelling pedlars, like Nightingale in Ben Jonson's *Bartholomew Fair* or Autolycus in *The Winter's Tale*, and like religious culture the influence of this form was felt throughout the country, not just by the London elite.
- Cultural forms available to aristocratic women included sewing and embroidery, both largely invisible today (though some very interesting embroidery by Mary Queen of Scots, with political meanings clearly visible, survives at Hardwick Hall in Derbyshire), and translation, such as the psalm translations of Mary Sidney.

All these, as noted above, are excluded from this chapter; and yet all are important elements within the culture from which arise the texts we *do* look at.

Visual art, architecture and gardens

At the climax of Book 2 of Edmund Spenser's poem *The Faerie Queene* (1590), Sir Guyon, the Knight of Temperance, is closing in on his quarry, Acrasia the enchantress. To get to where she is, the Bower of Bliss, he must first traverse the gardens around the Bower, full of natural and artificial delights. At one point, he finds that an overgrowing set of branches have

So fashioned a Porch with rare device,
Arched overhead with an embracing vine,

Whose bunches, hanging down, seemed to entice
All passers by to taste their luscious wine,
And did themselves into their hands incline,
As freely offering to be gathered:
Some deep empurpled as the hyacinth,
Some as the ruby, laughing sweetly red,
Some like faire emeralds, not yet well ripened.

(2.12.54)

Furthermore, we learn in the next stanza that this 'natural' scene has been improved by art: among these natural grapes, purple, red and green, someone has concealed artificial grapes made of burnished gold.

This bunch of grapes embodies three characteristic things about Renaissance English attitudes to visual art and, by extension, to art of all sorts, including writing. Firstly, the gold grapes are praised for being indistinguishable from the natural ones, just as in the extract above, the natural ones are praised for looking like artificial things – namely, polished gemstones of hyacinth (sapphire), ruby and emerald. So art is prized when it resembles nature, and yet nature is prized when it resembles art. This paradox is widespread through Renaissance literature, most obviously in pastoral poetry where 'melodious birds sing madrigals' and fruit hangs on trees 'like orange lamps in a green night' (Ferguson, 1996, 233, 433). But it also informs love sonnets which compare the lady's hair to golden wire, or Shakespeare's *The Winter's Tale*, where Leontes praises the statue of Hermione for being so lifelike as to make him almost think it is her.

Secondly, the passage from Spenser displays a characteristic Renaissance fascination with the difference between a simulation and the real thing: if something looks like a manmade structure, like the porch formed by the plants, but is not manmade, is it still a porch? Conversely, how can you tell from looking whether these are grapes or merely imitations of grapes? This interest in representation versus reality – seeming versus being – is one of the dominant notes of Renaissance culture. It informs, most famously, *Hamlet*, but also lies behind Marlowe's *Doctor Faustus*, which includes a representation of a devil-summoning ritual: how exactly is this different from a real devil-summoning ritual? Edward Alleyn, who first acted the part of Faustus, wore a cross round his neck when acting the role and speaking those lines, as an ostentatious sign that this ritual was unreal. In *The Winter's Tale*, the statue of Hermione turns out to be 'really' Hermione after all: and yet Hermione herself is not real, she is already only someone represented by a boy actor. Once you are into a world of representations, and plays-within-plays, where is 'real' reality to be found?

And this leads to the third point about this bunch of grapes: Sir Guyon destroys them. Surprisingly for the Knight of Temperance, once he has captured Acrasia, he systematically vandalizes, uproots and destroys everything in the garden, leaving it a ruined wasteland. This plot twist has been much discussed, but clearly part of the reason lies in Spenser's strong Protestantism. To this world-view, all forms of visual art – of visual beauty – are morally suspect, because they come between you and direct contemplation of the truly divine. In admiring them, you might find yourself committing idolatry, that is, worship of idols. The most extreme conclusion, which the poet Fulke Greville struggles with in his sonnet sequence *Caelica*, is that, since, in having an idea, you create a visual image in your brain, even thinking is potentially a form of idolatry. Renaissance Protestantism's most obvious dislike was visual art, the removal of which from churches – iconoclasm, literally the destruction of icons – was one of the major activities of the Reformation. Thereafter, religious paintings were indeed banned from churches (although more moderate Protestants, such as the poet George Herbert in his poem-sequence *The Temple*, were more receptive to beauty in churches). But throughout this period there is a simmering anxiety about whether all creative art is not inherently sinful.

This suspicion of visual art is why there were, overall, few pictures in early modern England, which has often been described as more of an aural than a visual culture. Portraits, especially miniature portraits, were in vogue, and could be given as luxury gifts, but painting collections were the preserve of the very rich. And whereas today many people know paintings at second hand through prints or reproductions, the opportunity for this was much more limited with Renaissance printing technology, in which even black-and-white engravings were rare and expensive. More energy went into architecture, especially the building of so-called 'prodigy houses', large, expensive new country houses which implicitly advertised the owner's wealth and modernity. These were often constructed by major landowners with a view to entertaining the monarch of the day, and of these Longleat in Wiltshire is one famous example. In the grounds of these prodigy houses, one would find landscaped gardens designed to be allegorically significant, filled with statues, grottoes and fountains that mixed the artificial and the natural. In a sense – and this is an indication of the fascinating tensions in Renaissance English culture – such gardens were built to create just the kind of environment which Sir Guyon must destroy.

The professional stage

Equally contradictory are early modern attitudes to theatre. On the one hand, theatrical performance was a central part of the educational system, as will be seen, and an important social custom inherited from the Middle Ages; on the other, theatre could be considered morally repugnant both in the abstract (since acting, after all, is a form of licensed lying) and in the flesh of its theatres (or its 'markets of bawdry', as the anti-theatrical campaigner Stephen Gosson called them).

To start, then, with the positive: Renaissance school education often privileged theatre, because theatre reflected one of its main concerns, the teaching of rhetorical and oratorical skills. This process started in the grammar school. There, the boys (for such education was all-male) had all their lessons conducted in Latin, and their educational exercises often took the form of dialogues or debates. In addition, among the literature they studied were the Latin comedies of Plautus and Terence, and the stilted but gory tragedies of Seneca. In comedies like *The Comedy of Errors* and tragedies like *Titus Andronicus*, Shakespeare wears these influences on his sleeve. At schools and universities these plays were not merely read but sometimes staged. Hence, drama and impersonation could be said to be at the heart of the Renaissance curriculum.

Alongside this classical Latin tradition of drama, filtered through schools, there was a medieval Christian tradition of drama which survived into the Renaissance period. As a rule, medieval drama can be divided into two categories: mystery plays and morality plays. Mystery plays, also known as 'cycle plays', were performed annually in larger towns such as York and Coventry. A cycle consists of a number of different short plays, which together narrate the biblical story from the creation of the world to its end at the Day of Judgement. Each of the numerous trade guilds in a city – the tanners, the carpenters, the butchers, and so on – would take on one play, cast it, and provide not merely the costumes but the decorated wagon from which the play was to be acted in the open streets around the town. On the designated day, all the wagons processed around the town, with their actors performing the same play at each of the different locations at which they stopped. Together, all the separate plays formed, in effect, one enormous day-long performance, so that a spectator staying at the same place throughout the day could see theatre on a truly epic scale. When one considers the Renaissance fashion for multi-part plays about the fate of a nation – the two parts of *Tamburlaine*, or of *Henry IV* – it seems likely that one model for that is provided by the memory of these mystery plays.

Morality plays, on the other hand, are stand-alone short dramas. In both the two best-known examples, *Everyman* and *Mankind*, the hero's name indicates his status not as an individual but as a symbolic representative of the whole human race. Our approach to drama tends nowadays to be conditioned by novels, and we expect believable characters with complex personalities, coherent pasts and hidden secrets, but such characters would have no place in the morality play. A consequence of the Reformation was the slow death of both morality and mystery plays, associated as they were with Catholicism. In London, and almost entirely restricted to London, a new invention came to fill some of the space that they had occupied: the permanent professional playhouse.

In these playhouses, acting companies were sponsored by a member of the royal family, or a high-ranking nobleman, although that is not to say that the sponsor had anything to do with the running of the company. The companies were business cooperatives, with close ties to the system of guilds. 'Sharers', such as Shakespeare, invested in the company and received in return a proportion of the profits: like everyone else, they had a vested interest in the company remaining profitable. The Globe, Shakespeare's main base throughout most of his career, could seat about 3,000 people. While attendance at the Globe was a fashionable luxury, the sheer success of the operation demonstrates that it was a luxury that many thousands were prepared to pay for. Similarly, while there is little direct information about how audiences behaved, it is clear that the atmosphere in a packed theatre could be electric – Nashe alludes to spectators shedding tears during tragedies, and one satirical comedy against the Spanish (Middleton's *A Game at Chess*) was so successful that it almost turned its audience into an anti-Spanish lynch mob. These facts are worth reviewing here because they speak to a common misconception held about Shakespeare's plays, namely, that they might consist of 'serious' scenes interspersed with low entertainment to keep the masses satisfied. Early modern theatre was indeed a commercial operation, and mass entertainment, but it does not therefore follow that Shakespeare and his colleagues were 'really' writing for an aristocratic audience, and having to include low entertainment for the common people. When Shakespeare or Jonson wrote explicitly for aristocrats, they did so in poems, or masques, and not in plays for the professional playhouse.

This question of professionalism is also relevant when it comes to considering how playtexts are preserved for us to read: almost exclusively in the form of early printings. But playing companies generally disliked letting their plays be printed, since that might diminish the pulling power of the play when staged. Certainly, the one surviving specimen of a contract drawn up between a company and a playwright – for the dramatist Richard Brome, who was writing in the reign of Charles I – specifies that he is not to print any of his plays without permission from the company. It also appears from this document that his duties involved writing new scenes to update old plays, a common Renaissance practice which might surprise modern readers accustomed to thinking of the author as a solitary creative genius, eager to see his vision translated faithfully into performance as purely as possible. But Renaissance theatre was often collaboratively composed, and often adjusted and updated in performance. The classic example of this process is Marlowe's *Dr Faustus*. Marlowe died in 1593, but the earliest surviving text of the play was printed in 1604, while another version, containing hundreds of substantial differences to lines, speeches and whole scenes, was printed in 1616. Both versions contain topical jokes which must have been written after Marlowe's death. Both versions are worth reading, and compelling in performance, but both are the product of a working theatre rather than of a solitary tortured individual playwright.

Broadly speaking, professional theatres came in two kinds: outdoor and indoor. The Globe is typical of an outdoor theatre, and is a useful example, partly because of its fame and partly because there exists a reconstruction, built in the 1990s on London's South Bank close to the site of the original, which makes it far easier to visualize. The location is the first important thing about the Globe: it was on the South Bank of the Thames, in an area then part of a 'liberty' or suburb called Bankside, which lay outside the city of London proper. Being on the far side of the river, the area was outside the jurisdiction of the city authorities, a fact which gave the theatre a certain limited freedom. In the same place, and for the same reasons, were to be found many of London's broth-els, and anti-theatrical campaigners often alleged that the prostitutes went to the theatre as a way of advertising them-selves to potential customers. The Globe was open-air and reliant on daylight for lighting, so performances took place in the afternoon. Whereas most modern theatres have a prosce-nium arch, which frames the action like a picture-frame or a television screen, with all the actors on one side of it and all the audience on the other, the Globe (like other early the-atres) had a thrust or 'apron' stage which projected into the audience. Most of that audience stood throughout the per-formance. Few props were used, and little, if any, scenery, although there was provision for some special effects, as the Globe, like most other theatres, seems to have had provision for a trapdoor, a 'discovery space' (a curtained area at the back of the stage from which the curtain could be drawn back) and a raised balcony. Music was provided by a house band of brass and woodwind instruments.

Indoor theatres such as the Blackfriars were, as the name suggests, large rooms set up as theatres and lit by candle-light. They offered a more intimate and exclusive venue, and gave the theatrical company more scope for making use of light-ing, music and rudimentary special effects. Shakespeare's late plays, which make extensive and innovative use of music and of special effects such as 'live' staged magic, are sometimes regarded as a move towards personal wisdom and serenity in the writer's old age; but it could just as well be argued that they reflect the opportunities thrown up by his company's new operation in the Blackfriars. If one is considering ques-tions of atmosphere and performance style in a Renaissance play, one of the first and most important questions is what type of theatre it was written for.

All the actors were British white males. No foreign charac-ter was truly foreign: Shakespeare's black hero Othello, con-stantly surprised by his own 'begrimed' skin, was played by a white actor in make-up. All the female characters were played by boys in their teens. It might be worth considering what effect this has on our reading of, say, *As You Like It*, in which

Rosalind is a girl who dresses up as a boy who impersonates a girl. In a sense, though, Rosalind remains a boy throughout – although such switches of gender make it difficult to pin down who Rosalind 'really' is. Some companies made this dissociation between the body of the actor and the body of the character even more obvious, in that they were 'boy companies' in which every part, male or female, adult or child, was taken by a boy actor.

Modern readers often ask whether a Renaissance audience could take such a theatre entirely seriously, when the actors are so patently not what they are pretending to be. The question is in one sense unanswerable, since such pretence lies, of course, at the heart of all drama. On the other hand, it is true that Renaissance plays are full of moments which draw attention to the nature of the dramatic illusion – 'metatheatrical' moments – such as Jacques' speech in *As You Like It* declaring to an audience packed into the Globe that 'all the world's a stage' (2.7.138), or Isabella's observation to the same audience in *Measure for Measure* that

> Man, proud man,
> Dressed in a little brief authority . . .
> Plays such fantastic tricks before high heaven
> As make the angels weep.
>
> (2.2.120–5)

Renaissance theatre is certainly full of characters who describe their lives as if they are theatre. This might be interpreted as a reflection on the unreality of Renaissance theatre, but it might better be described as indicating the extent to which metaphors of theatre permeated Renaissance imaginations of life as a whole.

Courtly performance

The Renaissance idea that 'all the world's a stage', and that all life might be considered a form of performance, is an interesting one to bring to the various forms of Renaissance courtly performance – forms such as processions, tournaments and masques – since in those forms performance itself was seen as a way of asserting one's power and one's place in the power relations of the court. For instance, during the reign of Queen Elizabeth, an important annual event was the Accession Day tilt, marking the day she ascended to the throne. In the 'tilt' – a tournament – Elizabeth's courtiers took part in jousting, an activity long redundant as a military exercise since military tactics now revolved around pikes and muskets rather than knights in armour. Rather, this consciously medievalist form of entertainment permitted courtiers to display their wit in ingenious choices of outfit, motto and design; their wealth; their manliness; and subtly nuanced displays of their loyalty to the Queen. Sir Guyon and his colleagues in shining armour in *The Faerie Queene* reflect no form of military reality, but they do reflect how Elizabethan aristocrats liked to think of themselves and display themselves in courtly performances.

Along with tournaments, the period also saw the emergence of the court masque as a cultural form. The court had long held a tradition of entertainments in which its members arrived in disguise, pretending to be visitors from distant lands: *Love's Labour's Lost* depicts such an entertainment, in which the young courtiers come in pretending to be Russians. But in the reign of King James, the masque developed into a multimedia event combining poetry, music, dance and elaborate scenes and machinery. Courtiers took parts in the masque, the plot of which, by convention, would hinge on a miraculous transformation achieved by the presence of the king. *The Masque of Blackness* is a good example, created by those great developers of the masque, Ben Jonson and the architect Inigo Jones, as a commission from James's wife Queen Anne, who wished to have an occasion to make herself up as a black woman, as was traditional in entertainments at the Scottish court. Jonson and Jones accordingly devised a plot in which the Queen and her retinue take the roles of African daughters of Niger, who have travelled to Britain because they have heard of the astonishing sun there.

To play this role, the Queen and her retinue made themselves up in blackface and wore exotic costume. The astonishing sun, of course, is revealed to be King James, who is present in the audience at the performance of the masque. James's influence, the masque says, is so wonderful that it can even blanch a black woman back to being white, thus explaining the eventual return of the Queen and her ladies to whiteness. This calculated display of subservience to James by the Queen and her retinue nevertheless stakes out a certain independence from him: a certain rejection of conventional ideas of femininity (since the Queen and her retinue have dared to dress themselves as Moors), and a willingness to make use of spectacle, when generally it was the King who used spectacle as a means of production of royal power.

There are, then, at least three reasons why the court masque is of particular interest to students of Renaissance theatre: first and foremost, the masques themselves are interesting texts; second, they are influential upon many works that imitate them, varying from the inset masque in *The Tempest* to John Milton's *Comus*, a regional masque staged for a wealthy aristocratic family; and third, because they indicate the power of drama as a tool to represent power, and therefore the potential subversiveness of the professional stage. In using all the techniques of theatre and spectacle, professional drama was dangerously close to the methods by which monarchs themselves ruled.

Other forms of performance which functioned, very clearly, as a means of negotiating power relations between the court and the city should also be mentioned. These were the various entertainments and series of speeches designed to greet monarchs at their coronations, when they first entered cities, or, in the case of Elizabeth I, when she went on progress. (It was Elizabeth's custom to go on 'progresses' – extended tours of the countryside – in the summer months, inviting herself and her very large retinue to stay with regional aristocrats.) Some of the most notable examples of these 'progress entertainments' include Sir Philip Sidney's *The Lady of May*, written to entertain Elizabeth I at Wanstead;

the entertainment written by George Gascoigne for the queen when she visited Kenilworth in 1575; the Elvetham entertainment, staged when she went on progress in 1591; the annual tilts (tournaments) held to celebrate Elizabeth's accession day, 17 November; and Richard Mulcaster's script for the mini-pageants attendant on her coronation (see Leahy, 2003). The effect of these is often difficult for us to reconstruct now because only the script survives, and the meanings of the events lay in many other elements, such as location, costume, music and the real identity of the performers. But they show, once again, the extent to which Renaissance power relations between monarch and court were often conducted through the medium of performance.

SOCIAL STRUCTURES

The structure of society

Renaissance society is often described as if it were a single, harmonious organization, part of the 'great chain of being' (see p. 24). In fact, it existed in a constant state of competition, renegotiation and reorganization. Nonetheless, as with the idea of the great chain of being, the model of the ordered and hierarchical society is quite a useful one to get started with for the purpose of establishing an initial perspective.

Any top-down account of early modern society would start with the monarch. The doctrine of the Divine Right of Kings – the idea that kings are more sacred than mere mortals – was one which was promoted, largely, by the monarchs themselves. For instance, the skin disease scrofula was also known as 'the King's evil', because it was believed that a touch of the monarch's hand could cure it. Charles I was particularly eager to take part in such ritual laying on of hands, which functioned partly as an assertion of his own holiness. Another, related, political idea was the theory of the King's Two Bodies, according to which the mortal body of the monarch was just a vessel for his or her 'body politic', defined by the Elizabethan lawyer Edward Plowden as 'a Body that cannot be seen or handled, consisting of policy and government', but which nonetheless somehow resided within the mortal body (Kantorowicz, 1997, 7). Hence Queen Elizabeth's famous declaration to her troops assembled to defend the country against the Spanish Armada that 'I may have the body of a weak and feeble woman, but I have the heart and stomach of a king' (Perry, 1990, 209) appropriates the political theory of the King's Two Bodies as a way of getting around the obstacle presented by her gender. In practice, all early modern monarchs worked hard at sustaining their power base among the senior aristocracy, and exercised a good proportion of their power through the institution of the 'court', the group of people who were at any time attending to them. In the Renaissance era, the court was almost invariably composed of a large group of the richest and most powerful aristocrats in the country. It was the most fashionable, most extravagant and, according to some observers, the most immoral place in Britain.

As for the senior aristocracy, one representative example of that class might be Robert Devereux, Earl of Essex (1565–1601), best remembered now for his failed rebellion against Elizabeth I. Essex's family had been wealthy for generations, and were part of a whole web of aristocratic families related by intermarriage. Their ancestral home was in Staffordshire, and Essex divided his time between estates in the country and the life of the court in London. As well as numerous servants, Essex's personal circle included a retinue of supporters, advisors and clients – almost, in effect, a miniature court of his own.

Below this level, there were two distinct types of rich person around London: gentry and citizens. Gentry can be thought of as, in a sense, scaled-down versions of the Earl of Essex, in that, in the usual course of events, they held their wealth in the form of lands in the areas outside London, normally inherited by birth or acquired by marriage. They would divide their time between their country estates, where they would hold a strong, almost feudal authority, over those who worked for them, and London, where they would attend court. As a rule of thumb, anyone with a knighthood or baronetcy – that is, anyone with the title 'Sir' – was a member of the gentry.

'Gentlemanly' and 'courtly' are words that have a moral charge in this period. 'Gentleman' profitably confuses ideas of ancestry (since 'gentle' literally refers to your family, to the stock from whom you originate), of wealth and status, and of behaviour. The modern usage of 'gentle' to mean 'considerate' or 'kindly' derives from this third, moral, flavour of the word 'gentleman' in the Renaissance period. Similarly, on a literal level 'courtly' implies that someone or something is associated with the court. However, courtliness often takes on a distinct moral tone, implying modern ideas of 'courtesy' and an ideal of good behaviour derived from Italian conduct books such as Baldessar Castiglione's *The Courtier* (1528), a series of dialogues in which characters discuss the nature of the perfect gentleman. Castiglione argues in particular for the importance of *sprezzatura* – a form of stylishness, in which a gentleman is able to combine a high level of accomplishment with an apparent lack of effort. In Britain, the poet and courtier Sir Philip Sidney came to symbolize this ideal of gentlemanliness or courtliness, one deriving from literary achievement and personal behaviour, not just from being of noble birth and attending court. Equally, by the opposite process, ideas of gentlemanliness and courtliness tend to imply that there *is* some sort of moral worthiness to being of noble birth and attending court: that courtiers are entitled to a sense of moral superiority over those from other social backgrounds.

All this provides an interesting light on Shakespeare's dissolute knights, such as Sir Toby Belch in *Twelfth Night*, or Sir John Falstaff, who features in *1 Henry IV*, *2 Henry IV* and *The Merry Wives of Windsor*. Falstaff spends his days in London taverns, among a group of common people and ne'er-do-wells, but his title indicates that he is one of the gentry. And when Falstaff is entrusted with a commission to raise a force of men to fight for King Henry IV (a classic gentry duty), he fails to fulfil his duty. He cheats both on raising the men, since he takes bribes to let the wealthier off from serving, and on buying them the proper equipment, with the result that his force is quickly massacred in the battle against the rebels. This is usually read as a moment when Falstaff fails a test of humanity, in that he lets down the people he works with and causes their deaths. But it might also be a moment when he fails in two of his primary duties as a gentleman, since he neither serves his king effectively, nor protects those lower down the social scale. Falstaff often behaves like a man of the people, but by birth he is one of the gentry: not one of us, but one of them.

Unlike the gentry, citizens generally had their homes in London, and derived their wealth (which could be very great) from trade of some sort rather than from owning land. They would not be invited to attend the court, and instead the main social organizations with which they were concerned were those of the city: the trade guilds, the city councils, the city militia and the lord mayor. Various literary forms, most of all the 'citizen comedies' of the London stage, record the aspirations, fears and values of this social group, the fore-runners of today's middle classes.

The citizens' trade guilds can be most typically illustrated by an example: the goldsmiths' guild was a cooperative organization to which belonged all the goldsmiths of the city. The guild regulated the behaviour of members of the profession, and also represented the interests of the gold-smithing trade to the Lord Mayor and to other centres of power in London. In addition, they sponsored entertainments, engaged in charity work and regulated the apprentice system, a staple of citizen life. In this system, after a basic education, a young man would be indentured as an apprentice for a term of seven years to a master who was already 'free of' a certain trade – that is to say, a fully accredited member of, as it may be, the goldsmiths' guild. Over the next seven years, the apprentice would learn that trade as an employee of his master, often living in his master's house, so that, if all went well, at the end of that period the apprentice himself would become a full member of the guild. Many apprentices married their master's daughter, or widow, and took over the business built up by their master. In a poem to his younger colleague Richard Brome, Ben Jonson wrote that Brome had served 'a prenticeship, which few do nowadays': for Jonson in this poem, artists are not divinely inspired, priest-like figures, but apprentices learning their craft.

On the one hand, buoyed by their sense of moral superiority, courtiers tended to deride citizens as unfashionable and vulgar. From the citizens' point of view, conversely, the stereotype of the courtier was of an extravagant spendthrift, likely to be a bad payer of his debts. Citizens were associated with a different set of moral norms, which praised qualities like hard work, thrift and honesty. As a general rule, citizens were also perceived to be more sympathetic than the gentry to Puritanism, although this is far from being a hard-and-fast rule. Jonson, Marston and Chapman's 'citizen comedy' *Eastward Ho* demonstrates typical 'citizen' values in the character of Golding, who is a dutiful apprentice to his master, Touchstone, and ends the play married to Touchstone's daughter. But it also suggests that not all members of the apprentice class shared the values of Golding: for instance, Golding's fellow apprentice Quicksilver is looking to get rich quickly and to live the high life, an aspiration punished within the play by an appropriate humiliation.

Below this social rank, the poorer residents of London are relatively little visible in literature except when a 'mob' is represented, as in, for instance, Shakespeare's *Coriolanus*. Equally invisible are the poorer residents of the countryside, who when they do appear in literature are written off as 'churls' or 'clowns' – that is, ignorant peasants. Servants, however, constitute something of a special case, and require separate discussion.

The point about servants is that, as the foregoing discussion has implied, the whole of Renaissance society is implicated in 'service' of some sort: local gentry serve their regional superiors, even higher aristocracy are servants of the monarch, and in that even monarchs are seen as 'God's lieutenants', they, too, are perceived as servants to God, the master of the ultimate household. Hence, a certain dignity attaches to the role of household servant. In addition, because the Petrarchan tradition figures a lover as a servant to his mistress, there is an association between the role of servant and the role of lover exemplified in Shakespeare's Viola or in this verse by a little-known servant poet of the 1580s, James Yates:

> A Lady I obey and serve
> With heart and mind and only will,
> Who hath done more then I deserve,
> For which I am her servant still,
> To wish her well, since wealth is small,
> And wishing is the most of all.
>
> (Yates, 1582, M2r)

Indeed, important gentry might have less important gentry as servants: for example, in *Twelfth Night* Maria is a 'waiting-gentlewoman'. In Renaissance drama, some servants subvert the social order, like De Flores in Middleton and Rowley's *The Changeling*. De Flores starts off merely as the servant of his mistress, but in the course of the play, as he helps her slip into evil, he becomes, as her assistant, her lover, her blackmailer and eventually her killer. But other servants are seen as the guardians of the social order, like the servant in *King Lear* who attempts to prevent his master Cornwall from blinding Gloucester:

> Hold your hand, my lord:
> I have served you ever since I was a child;
> But better service have I never done you
> Than now to bid you hold.
>
> (3.7.73–6)

In either case, the idea of service is a powerful one in Renaissance culture.

There were, of course, many mechanisms for social mobility. One of the most direct was intermarriage, and many citizen comedies revolve around wealthy citizen parents who wish to marry their daughter to someone of gentry stock, even if in other respects they are entirely unsuitable. Alternatively, citizens could make an application for a coat of arms, a transaction which usually involved significant expense and perhaps the 'finding' of a fictitious ancestor or two. The best-known citizens to take advantage of this route to gentry status were, of course, the Shakespeare family, since William's father, John, successfully applied for a grant of arms via this route in 1596. Yet another route was through education, since all university graduates were considered to be gentlemen by virtue of having done a degree: as the upwardly mobile flatterer Baldock boasts in Marlowe's *Edward II*, while he does not have a coat of arms, 'my gentry/ I fetched from Oxford, not from heraldry' (2.2.242–3).

Baldock's line expresses, in a sentence, the main tension with which this section has been concerned: the question of whether social status reflects inborn qualities or merely accidents of upbringing. In a sense, this debate is closely linked to the Renaissance tensions between Art and Nature discussed on pages 31–4, although there is something of a Catch-22 flavour to it, since if you believe that Nature is more powerful than Art, aristocrats can argue that they are rightfully born to rule, whereas if you believe in Art, aristocrats can argue that they are uniquely fitted to rule by virtue of their gentlemanly upbringing. The early modern rhetoric of an ordered, stable society in which the right people are conveniently born in the right social positions is in a continuing, ongoing and fascinating dialogue with the rhetoric we see used by Edmund in *King Lear*, in which social power is ripe for the taking even by those who lack social legitimation: 'Now, Gods, stand up for bastards' (1.2.22).

The family

The Renaissance family looked very different from our modern nuclear one. As will be discussed below (pp. 109–10), people in Renaissance England acknowledged relationships at far greater degrees of distance than we do now. They also had many more immediate family members than we are likely to have. Any forms of contraception that did exist were extremely crude and not widely available or used and, consequently, large families were the norm. (If you go into a church which dates back to the sixteenth century or before, you will often see tombs of Elizabethan couples with numerous little figures of all their children at their feet, girls on one side and boys on the other.) Childbirth was a risky business: female anatomy was still imperfectly understood (the womb, for instance, was popularly supposed to be able to wander round the body, as well as being thought to be the source of hysteria), and it has been estimated that a woman had a one in three chance of dying with every pregnancy. Expectant mothers often wrote letters of spiritual advice for their offspring, such as Elizabeth Joscelin's *The Mother's Legacy* (1624), because they knew that they might not survive the birth.

In theory, married life could begin much earlier than it does now. The age of consent was 12 for girls and 14 for boys, who were thought to be more delicate than girls and liable to be damaged by having sexual intercourse too early (Shakespeare's Juliet is just coming up to her 14th birthday, and her mother observes that when she was the same age as her daughter is now, she was already a mother). However, very few couples actually married this early. It was more usual to wait until the early or even the mid-twenties, particularly in the case of poorer people, who did not marry until they could afford to do so. Shakespeare himself was only 18 when he married Anne Hathaway, but she was 26. Like many others at the time, their wedding was hastened by the fact that the bride was pregnant. In rural societies, indeed, it was customary until a much later period for a couple not to marry until the bride-to-be had demonstrated her fertility by conceiving.

Aristocratic couples, for whom finances were not an issue, were more likely to marry younger. (Perhaps the most extreme example of this is Richard, Duke of York, the

younger of the two princes in the Tower, who was already a
widower when he died at the age of 8.) Aristocratic matches
were generally (though not always) arranged by the couple's
families, and often the couple would be 'betrothed' or 'contracted' for a considerable time before the actual wedding.
There was much uncertainty in the period over the precise
legal status of such 'pre-contracts' and how binding they
were. At the heart of Renaissance marriage law lay the doctrine of consent. In theory, all that was necessary for a valid
ceremony of marriage was for both parties to express consent
in front of a witness: in Shakespeare's *The Taming of the Shrew*,
for instance, Biondello observes that 'I knew a wench
married in an afternoon as she went to the garden for parsley
to stuff a rabbit' (4.4.97–9).

Such private ceremonies could be conducted in two ways,
known respectively as *sponsalia per verba de praesenti* ('spousals
through words of the present') and *sponsalia per verba de futuro*
('spousals through words of the future'). The first – and
simpler – of these is well illustrated by John Webster's 1613
play *The Duchess of Malfi*, where the Duchess marries Antonio
in her bedchamber with only her maid Cariola as witness
and then asks, 'What can the church force more?' (1.1.488).
The added complication was that in the case of a contract
being made for the future, this actually became permanently,
legally binding if the couple then consummated the marriage (i.e. had sex). This is the situation in Shakespeare's
Measure for Measure, where Angelo and Mariana had been
pre-contracted, and so the Duke assures Isabella that it is 'no
sin' for Mariana to take her place in the bed-trick, for by
sleeping with Angelo she will automatically become his wife.

However, the uncertainties surrounding such marriages
could be extremely problematic: Church courts were clogged
with disputes about whether X really had promised to marry
Y. Perhaps the dangers of the private marriage are best illustrated by the case of Lady Catherine Grey, younger sister of
the nine days' queen Lady Jane Grey, who secretly married
the Earl of Hertford. Already dangerous because Lady
Catherine, as a great-niece of Henry VIII, had a potential

claim to the throne, this move proved to have tragic consequences when the only witness, the earl's sister, died, and neither the earl nor Lady Catherine could remember the name of the priest who had married them. Elizabeth, refusing to believe that they were really married at all, imprisoned them both as soon as it became obvious that Lady Catherine was pregnant. After bearing the earl two sons, Lady Catherine died, and the earl had to campaign furiously to have the legitimacy of his sons confirmed.

As a result of this and other cases, there was increasing pressure for marriages to be contracted and celebrated in public. Although the answer to the Duchess of Malfi's question 'What can the church force more?' was still technically 'Nothing', throughout the period there was growing worry about the status of pre-contracts, and it is notable that at the end of *Measure for Measure* the Duke still tells Angelo to take Mariana away and marry her, even though they might well be understood by many in the audience to be already married by virtue of having consummated a pre-contract.

Once a marriage had unquestionably occurred, it was definitively and unquestioningly understood that the husband was superior to the wife. He was the head of the household, and, in a sense, his wife's head too: 'The husband is head of the wife' said St Paul (Ephesians 5.23), and no one in the Renaissance would have been likely to disagree. Since woman was burdened with the curse of Eve, she was inferior to man physically, morally, intellectually and spiritually, it was thought, and he had to be her guide and guardian. Some Protestant divines even suggested that women should confess their sins to their husbands as they would once have done to a priest, since woman's nature was too weak to allow her to deal with God without an intermediary. There was, however, also growing emphasis on what is often called 'companionate marriage', that is, on the husband and wife providing affection and companionship for each other, and on the wife acting as a helpmate for her husband. Hence it was commonly thought in the period that, certainly compared with the Continent, England was something of a paradise for women.

Another major difference between Renaissance times and ours was the importance of servants not just in society, as seen above, but in the household. Indeed the term 'family' was generally applied not just to the husband, wife and children, but also to their servants, who took an active and interested part in all the affairs of the household, even those which we might suppose were not their province. In Thomas Heywood's 1603 play *A Woman Killed with Kindness*, for example, it is one of the servants, Nick, who is the first to observe the adultery of the mistress of the house, and he immediately tells his master and accompanies him on his errand to detect the guilty couple, while in Shakespeare's *The Taming of the Shrew* the servants are active participants in Petruchio's campaign to tame Katherine. A Renaissance family, then, was likely to be a much larger and more complex organization than we would probably now think of as a family, and it was indeed conceived of not just as a private unit but effectively as a microcosm of the larger state, with the husband/master as king of his own private domain. Thus, for a servant to kill his master or a wife her husband, as Alice Arden does in the anonymous domestic tragedy *Arden of Faversham*, was actually 'petty treason', a smaller-scale, but not less serious, version of the crime of treason against a monarch. When we are reading Renaissance writing about the family, therefore, it is always wise to remember that public as well as private issues may be at stake.

We may also find that it is in the matter of family affairs that Renaissance literature can sometimes seem most strange to us, because this is an area with which we are ourselves familiar and which we may therefore assume we ought to recognize when it is depicted in literature. Customs and concepts of family life have changed, however. In Shakespeare's *Romeo and Juliet*, Juliet's parents are completely unsympathetic to her unwillingness to marry Count Paris: they – particularly her father – expect unquestioning obedience from their daughter. Children were indeed regarded as effectively possessions of their parents; they were, for instance, required to kneel and ask their parents' blessings, in a formal gesture of respect. Some historians have even argued that because child mortality was so high parents did not put as much emotional investment into their children as they do now, at least not when they were very young and before it had become clear that they would survive, and there certainly seems to be something offhand about the casual remark inserted at the end of a long letter from Sir William Lower to his friend Thomas Harriot in 1611: 'My wife is well. Now you know all my comforts. I have lost my second boy also, and well near eighty cattle of the murrain, and the [sic] die still; now you know all my discomforts and losses' (Rukeyser, 1970, 224). What does seem clear, though, is that relations between siblings, especially brothers and sisters, could be very close: when Prince Henry, eldest son of James VI/I, lay dying in 1612, his last words were 'Where is my dear sister?' (Strong, 1986, 221).

One aspect of Renaissance family life which may well (indeed one hopes it does) seem particularly strange to us is the virtually universal male paranoia about the possibility of female infidelity. On the evidence of the plays, poems and prose romances of the period, the entire culture would seem to be suffering from what modern psychiatrists have diagnosed as an 'Othello' syndrome – that is, an obsessive and ungrounded fear of being cuckolded. (The female equivalent of cuckold, 'cuckquean', is much more rarely used.) Literary and non-literary writing alike abounds in tags and proverbs which casually dismiss and demonize all women as likely to be unfaithful – 'casta est quam nemo rogavit' ('she is chaste whom no one has asked', i.e. the only woman who has not strayed is one who has not yet been propositioned). In Thomas Heywood's domestic tragedy *A Woman Killed with Kindness*, for instance, the heroine, Anne Frankford, is approached by her husband's best friend, Wendoll, who declares that he wishes to sleep with her. After a moment's delay, during which she announces that she fears for her soul if she does this, Anne agrees. She has shown no previous sign either of discontent in her marriage or of attraction to Wendoll – but she has been asked, so she agrees. This scene might now look to us like a psychological failure on Heywood's part as a dramatist, but it is all too likely that his original audience noticed no inadequacy in his representation of the likely course of events.

So widespread was the fear of cuckoldry that a number of rituals and beliefs accrued to it. Most notably, men whose wives had been unfaithful to them were said to have been 'horned' (to make the point that betrayal was universal, Michelangelo represented even his Moses with cuckold's horns on the tomb of Pope Julius II). Horn jokes are thus a never-failing source of entertainment in Renaissance literature, although they can all too easily turn to tragedy, as when Othello, convinced that his wife is deceiving him, rubs his forehead to see if his horns have sprouted yet.

It is not really clear why there should have been such a cultural obsession with the idea of cuckoldry. Partly it can be attributed to the general belief in the frailty of women, but modern historians have also suggested that it should be seen as rooted in the rise of capitalism, and the concentration of property within a nuclear family leading to men being increasingly anxious that the children to whom they transmitted their property should be their own. (It was generally believed that the father was solely responsible for transmitting the characteristics and personality of the child; the mother was seen as providing merely the physical material from which its body was shaped.) It should also be remembered that although Andreas Vesalius had shed considerable light on the workings of the womb in 1543, the biological processes of conception and birth remained deeply mysterious and a site of anxiety. Whatever the reason, the idea of all women's potential for infidelity is a constant in Renaissance writing.

2

Literature in the Renaissance

MAJOR GENRES

This chapter is divided into four sections. The first three cover poetry, drama and prose, in that order, each divided into subsections by genre; the fourth considers four literary movements that might be particularly relevant to students.

POETRY

Renaissance poetry can be organized into genres, and this chapter considers four of the most important and distinctive: lyric, pastoral, epic and satire.

Lyric

Modern lyric poetry is often assessed in terms of its 'authenticity' – how well the poet conveys the emotions which they have felt. Such criteria of authenticity are hard to work with in the case of Renaissance poems, since they are often anonymous, or by writers to whose inner life we have no sort of access. Just as a song does not necessarily reveal the state of mind of the singer, so a lyric poem does not give one access into the mind of the poet – merely into the mind of the speaker whom the poet creates. This is particularly true of Renaissance lyric poetry, as Shakespeare's Sonnet 130 demonstrates:

> My mistress' eyes are nothing like the sun;
> Coral is far more red than her lips' red:
> If snow be white, why then her breasts are dun [*brown*];
> If hairs be wires, black wires grow on her head.
> I have seen roses damask'd [*patterned*], red and white,
> But no such roses see I in her cheeks;
> And in some perfumes is there more delight
> Than in the breath that from my mistress reeks.
> I love to hear her speak, yet well I know
> That music hath a far more pleasing sound;
> I grant I never saw a goddess go –
> My mistress, when she walks, treads on the ground.
> And yet, by heaven, I think my love as rare
> As any she [*woman*], belied with false compare [*comparison*].

Any reader of poetry ancient or modern will recognize that this poem breaks an important convention, which is that love poetry is complimentary in its description of the beloved. In particular, a more experienced reader will notice that this poem is a sonnet, a literary form as distinct, in its way, as a limerick.

How do we know that this poem is a sonnet? It is 14 lines long, the traditional length of the sonnet. It has the rhyme scheme ABABCDCDEFEFGG. A rhyme scheme uses a letter for each line of the poem, showing which other lines it rhymes with. In this poem, the first line's 'sun' rhymes with the third line's 'dun'; and the second line's 'red' with the fourth line's 'head', so that the first four lines of this poem are described as rhyming ABAB. This process is continued on through the poem until the 13th and 14th lines, which rhyme with each other, and are represented as GG in the rhyme scheme above. If one works through Shakespeare's sonnets, applying this test to each of them, a large majority of them turn out to have exactly this rhyme scheme through their 14 lines. So this poem is not the spontaneous overflow of unique emotions: it comes off a production line along with a number of other poems of the same shape and form.

Nor was Shakespeare the only Renaissance author to write sequences of sonnets: the sonnet, and the sonnet sequence, were among the most popular literary forms of the Renaissance, and carried along with them a whole repertoire of characteristic literary devices. For instance, a feature common in sonnets is the 'blazon' – a list which describes the beloved's face and body feature by feature, with a stress on their likeness to fair and beautiful things – and one could say that Shakespeare's poem both partakes of and reacts against such a convention. (Spenser's *Amoretti* 15 is a classic example of a 'straight' blazon of a woman's body, though even this has a twist in it, praising the woman's beautiful body but ultimately celebrating instead her mind.)

So can this lyric be taken as offering an access into the mind of William Shakespeare as he chooses to reject convention and instead tell the truth about his love? Unfortunately not. The 'contreblazon' – an insulting version of the blazon – is itself already a literary convention at the time that Shakespeare is writing, the constant process of rejecting previous literary conventions itself making new conventions as it goes. This sonnet's charm depends on giving you the illusion of access to Shakespeare's mind, but it is also a highly conventional poem.

Conventions, then, are crucial to understanding poetry, and the most important of these for lyric poetry such as Shakespeare's sonnets is Petrarchanism, a style modelled loosely on the work of the Italian poet Petrarch (1304–74), and in particular on his sequence of sonnets and other poems, *Canzoniere*. The situation outlined in this sequence is as follows: the speaker is in love with a woman, Laura, whom he hardly knows. The woman is far superior to him in social class; she is herself a paragon of chaste virtue; and she does not return his love for her. He loves her, or he loves the idea of her, to the point of religious adoration. Indeed, during the sonnet sequence Laura dies, causing a religious conversion in the speaker of the *Canzoniere*, who converts his love for Laura into love for God. Another legacy of Petrarchanism is that, as sexual love is often figured as a form of religious love, so religious love can be figured in poems in terms that make it resemble sexual love.

At the court of Henry VIII, a group of poets including Sir Thomas Wyatt and Henry Howard, Earl of Surrey, appropriated Petrarchan themes and style, even in some cases writing poems which were direct translations from Petrarch's Italian. So, one of the things that makes 'They flee from me', the Thomas Wyatt poem discussed in the Chapter 1, so striking is that it is unusual and unexpected among Wyatt's poems in depicting a woman taking the sexual initiative: 'When her loose gown from her shoulders did fall,/And she me caught in her arms . . .' (Ferguson, 1996, 115). This change of convention is startlingly effective, read in the context of the other work of Wyatt and his contemporaries, which generally features classically Petrarchan ardent men and chaste and unattainable women. But Petrarchan poetry really came into its own during the reign of Queen Elizabeth, in part because Elizabeth liked to figure her courtiers' utter dependence on her as a form of courtly love-relationship, so that the relationship of a courtier to the Queen was easily assimilated to the relationship between the Petrarchan lover and his permanently unattainable beloved. Elizabethan men spent a lot of time thinking about the sensation of being a servant to an all-powerful woman.

The Elizabethan sonneteers – of whom Sir Philip Sidney and Edmund Spenser are the best-known examples – took over the Petrarchan tradition and rang a series of changes on it, developing a narrative over the course of a sequence of sonnets. Spenser's *Amoretti*, for instance, moves towards the marriage of the speaker to his beloved; Sidney's *Astrophil and Stella*, seemingly at least in part inspired by an adulterous relationship with the noblewoman Penelope, Lady Rich, experiments with making the addressee faithless. Shakespeare's sonnets, the most famous example of the type, are at least in part addressed to a man. In fact, one might say that Shakespeare's sonnets play games with the idea of narrative within a sonnet sequence, since, while narrative fragments can apparently be discerned, no clear and coherent pattern can be drawn over them all. The speaker of the sonnets has a complex and conflicted love-relationship with a beautiful young man; he also addresses several poems, such as Sonnet 130, to a 'Dark Lady'; a rival poet is mentioned in several poems. Much critical ink has been expended on the question of attempting to identify these characters with identifiable historical figures, and on determining which poems belong to which character. But regardless of the historical truth or otherwise of these claims, what is clear is that one powerful way to understand Shakespeare's sonnets is by comparing other Renaissance love poems, to understand the conventions at work. Indeed, given that Renaissance lyric is so largely a matter of conventions, its constant surprise is that it can speak so powerfully from those conventions to readers of the present day.

The foregoing discussion has concentrated on love lyric, but in doing so has so far omitted the other great preoccupation of Renaissance lyric: religion. Indeed, as noted above, the Petrarchan tradition treats sexual love as a form of religion; and religion, sometimes, almost as a form of sexual love, which results in lyrics like John Donne's 'Batter my heart, three person'd God', in which God is imagined as a lover asked to take possession of the speaker's body and soul. Donne develops the paradox towards a daring conclusion, asking God to

> Take me to you, imprison me, for I,
> Except [*unless*] you enthrall me, never shall be free,
> Nor ever chaste, except you ravish me.
>
> (Ferguson, 1996, 289)

In this sonnet, God's love is a force imagined in explicitly sexual terms. On the other hand, not all imaginations of God in lyric poetry of the period share the explicitly sexual vision of this poem, and in their variety one can see something of the extent to which religious thought permeated all aspects of people's lives. For instance, George Herbert's poem 'Redemption' develops a riddle-like extended comparison between human sinfulness and the unexpectedly mundane topic of land rental. The speaker has 'been tenant long to a rich lord' – that is, God – but, 'not thriving', realizes he needs the lord to cancel his existing obligations and make a new lease. The twist is that the 'rich lord' is not to be found 'in heaven at his manor', but instead among 'a ragged noise and mirth / Of thieves and murderers', where he dies even in granting the tenant his request for a new lease (Ferguson, 1996, 329–30). The 'rich Lord', then, is God, and the death among thieves and murderers corresponds to Jesus' death on the cross. In this lyric, religious mystery is figured in an analogy drawn from landholding law. While Petrarchanism, in all its forms, is an influential force in Renaissance lyric poetry, it can operate in other modes as well.

Pastoral

After Petrarchanism, perhaps the second most important convention of early modern poetry is pastoral. At its simplest, the pastoral boils down to three main ideas, the first of which is that the pastoral is set in the countryside. In particular, shepherds and shepherdesses are a strong indication of pastoral, and a singing shepherd is absolutely typical, since the pastoral convention sees all shepherds as surrogate poets; but other professions, such as fishermen and mowers, can also make appearances within pastoral, and all that is really necessary is that the poems be set in the countryside. Secondly, the countryside where the poem is set is described as an ideal, unspoilt place, beautiful to look upon, where the stresses of city life do not apply. This connects Renaissance pastoral back to the classical Greek idea of the Golden Age, an imagined time before men's crimes made the world dangerous and unpleasant; or back, alternatively, to the Bible's representation of the same idea in the Garden of Eden, a place which was an earthly Paradise, but from which mankind is now exiled because of Adam and Eve's sin. And this is the third and most important thing about the pastoral: it is always written from a position of exile. Writers of pastoral are not themselves shepherds, and the countryside is always being described by a poet writing in the city. All concerned, writers and readers alike, know this. Hence, a sense of deliberate artificiality, entirely at odds with the content which praises nature for its simplicity and immediacy, is part of the convention. Nature is praised, but in a consciously artful way.

For example, one could use as a test case for these three ideas the opening lines of Christopher Marlowe's lyric 'The Passionate Shepherd to his Love':

Come live with me and be my love,
And we will all the pleasures prove [*try*]
That valleys, groves, and hills and fields,
Woods, or steepy mountain yields.

And we will sit upon the rocks,
Seeing the shepherds feed their flocks
By shallow rivers, to whose falls
Melodious birds sing madrigals.

And I will make thee beds of roses
And a thousand fragrant posies,
A cap of flowers, and a kirtle [*gown*]
Embroidered all with leaves of myrtle;

A gown made of the finest wool
Which from our pretty lambs we pull;
Fair lined slippers for the cold,
With buckles of the purest gold.

(Ferguson, 1996, 233)

This is certainly set in the countryside, and has shepherds in it, one of whom – as the poem's title informs us – is speaking the poem. We are thus on safe ground in saying that this is a pastoral poem according to the first of the criteria above, and we might look to read it in terms of the second and third. The countryside is indeed idealized, since it offers 'pleasures' of many different sorts. Flowers are plentiful, and the shepherd and his love appear to have plenty of leisure time, rather than needing to spend all their time earning a living. (This idea of *otium*, or leisure, is an ideal particularly associated with classical pastoral.)

And yet, even on the evidence of the first few lines, the countryside that these characters inhabit might not strike us as entirely realistic. Lines 3–4 enumerate various different sorts of scenery, without lingering on any one, so that you would be hard put to say whereabouts in the world this landscape is. Lines 4–8 describe a strange location where woodland, meadows and rocky waterfall all co-exist. Ideas of Art and Nature start to get more complicated as Marlowe's shepherd makes clothing from plants, and embroiders representations of plants onto clothing. The generic 'rules' of pastoral give us a toolkit with which to read this poem, by asking us to pay particular attention to the realism or otherwise of the poem; the slippers of the fourth stanza, which appear to be improvised by pulling fleece from the lambs, are nonetheless embellished with buckles of pure gold, implying both wealth and forethought. One might conclude, especially in the light of the title distancing the poet from the speaker, that part of the point of this poem is the contrast between the simplicity it offers and the sophistication with which it is written and read.

But pastoral, like Petrarchanism, is not a completely static set of conventions, but an evolving genre where each poem trades on its difference from previous poems in the genre. The most obvious example of this evolution relates to religion. Renaissance pastoral looks back to classical models, most importantly the *Eclogues* of Virgil, short poems written in Latin in the first century BC. The *Eclogues*, ten poems in which shepherds have singing contests with one another or mourn dead friends or describe their unhappy love lives, were taught as a set text in almost all medieval and Renaissance schools and were hugely influential. An obvious problem for those teachers was that Virgil himself was not a Christian: however, various manoeuvres were possible in order to get round this problem, including reading the poems as allegories of Christianity, written by someone who meant well but who died before Christ himself came to earth to save mankind. (On allegories, see below, p. 119–20). In particular, Virgil's 'Messianic Eclogue', which predicted the coming of a new Golden Age, was often taken as a garbled prediction of the arrival of Christ, and hence pastoral could be seen as a religious form of poetry. For Christian writers, pastoral is rich in such possibilities: as well as potentially representing the poet, the shepherd could represent Christ himself (since 'the Lord is my shepherd'), or a priest, a 'pastor' (literally, a shepherd) looking after his 'flock' of worshippers. Certainly, Milton's pastoral poem *Lycidas* (published in its first version in 1638) works like this, with the lazy shepherds in that poem representing both bad poets and a recognizable type of 1630s priest considered by Milton to be insufficiently zealous in their Protestantism: 'The hungry sheep look up, and are not fed' (Ferguson, 1996, 357). Milton takes aim here particularly at the moderate Anglicanism associated with Archbishop Laud. For Milton, such an approach is laziness to the point of recklessness, and *Lycidas* threatens that such lazy shepherds will come to grief. With the outbreak of the Civil War in 1642, Laudian priests were indeed removed from power and, republishing the poem in 1645, Milton added a headnote explaining that the poem 'fortells the ruin of our corrupted clergy then in their height', and making its veiled political import explicit. Hence, pastoral poems, although set in a deliberately unreal world, can also be intensely political as they react to and modify the conventions of the genre.

This idea of pastoral as an evolving dialogue can be further illustrated by returning briefly to Marlowe's 'Come Live With Me', which prompted an imitation or parody,

John Donne's poem 'The Bait', in which the motif of shepherding is replaced by a series of images taken from fishing, as can be seen from the first stanza:

> Come live with me, and be my love,
> And we will some new pleasures prove
> Of golden sands, and crystal brooks,
> With silken lines and silver hooks.

Marlowe's poem also prompted 'The Nymph's Reply to the Shepherd', written probably by Sir Walter Ralegh, which begins:

> If all the world and love were young,
> And truth in every shepherd's tongue,
> These pretty pleasures might me move
> To live with thee and be thy love . . .

> (Ferguson, 1996, 140)

The nymph goes on to outline a countryside which is the opposite of the pastoral world. In the nymph's world, 'Time drives the flocks from field to fold / When rivers rage and rocks grow cold'. Hostile weather and the relentless passing of time are both aspects of the countryside which are not normally considered in pastoral, so that this poem might be considered 'antipastoral', even while it takes several words directly from Marlowe's first two stanzas – 'flocks', 'field[s]', 'rocks' and 'rivers' – and turns round their meaning. Just as the Petrarchan idea of the blazon can be turned round and made into a contreblazon, while still recognizably within the Petrarachan tradition, so a poem such as Ralegh's 'The Nymph's Reply' can be recognizably antipastoral even while still belonging to a pastoral tradition.

Epic

As with Petrarchan and pastoral conventions, so with epic conventions: what we see in this Renaissance poetic genre is a constant process of reworking ideas and motifs from previous poems. Epic was seen by Renaissance writers as the most important of all genres, the master genre that contained elements of all the others. Epic poems are long; they typically deal with the fate of a nation, rather than just an individual, although they have at their heart an 'epic hero' who carries the fate of the nation in his hands; they have a cast of thousands; and they are written in a high and grand poetic style. Within that basic framework, however, there is a constant stream of developments, refinements and reinventions.

Comparison of three epics will indicate something of these developments. The first is Virgil's *Aeneid*, written in Latin in the years leading up to his death in 19 BC. For Virgil, as for his imitators Spenser and Milton, writing an epic was the ultimate achievement of a poetic career: one serves one's apprenticeship in shorter genres, particularly pastoral, and concludes one's life by writing an epic masterpiece to rival, in Virgil's case, predecessors including the Greek epic writer Homer. The *Aeneid* tells the story of Aeneas, a Trojan refugee from the Greek siege of Troy described by Homer, who wanders the Mediterranean until he eventually lands in Italy and founds the nation that will one day become the Roman Empire within which and for which Virgil was writing. Along the way, his adventures include a trip down to the underworld (hell); a doomed love-affair with the African Queen Dido; and many scenes of massed battle between the Trojan settlers and the native Italians.

Many of the same ingredients, such as massed battles, love affairs, and a trip down to the underworld, occur in Edmund Spenser's epic poem *The Faerie Queene*. Spenser's imitations of Virgil are filtered through the tradition of romance, the dominant form of long narrative in the medieval period. 'Romance' is a word which has since acquired other connotations, but medieval and Renaissance romance is readily identifiable even now by its contents: wandering knights on quests, fair maidens, magic and dragons. Anything with dragons in it is a descendant, of some sort, of medieval and Renaissance romance. Romance also has a characteristic structure: long, rambling and often incomplete (as *The Faerie Queene* is, breaking down only a quarter of the way into its proposed 24 books), which contrasts with the more obviously patterned story of the *Aeneid* or *Paradise Lost*.

Book I of *The Faerie Queene* describes the adventures of a knight with no name, usually referred to as the Redcross Knight because of the insignia on his shield – a red cross on a white silver background, both a Christian symbol and the emblem of England still to be seen at international sporting events. Spenser describes his poem as an 'allegory, or dark conceit', so that one is invited to read Redcross as an allegory, a representative of something bigger than himself: of all Englishmen, perhaps, or even of all right-thinking Christians (Spenser, 1977, 737). His mission, we learn, is to find and kill the dragon that threatens the kingdom of the fair maiden Una, and one of the first things he does is to kill a scaly monster which Una says is called Error. By the same logic that makes Redcross into an allegory of all Englishmen, it might appear that the monster Error is an allegory of error in general, and that by killing Error, Redcross has ensured that he will not suffer from errors thereafter. It turns out, however, that in Spenser's world, allegorically killing Error is not the same as making yourself proof against errors, since immediately after the fight, Redcross makes a series of bad decisions that nearly cost him his life. With each new twist the reader is asked to reassess what they already know about the Faerie Land where the poem takes place, and about what each of the characters in the poem might represent. The reader, like Redcross, experiences the sensation of trying to make sense of a vast and endless world which seems to work on many different levels at once: a classic example of epic fullness and complexity.

Whereas *The Faerie Queene* achieves epic fullness by this sense of an extended, rambling world inviting endless exploration, Milton's *Paradise Lost*, written 80 years later, seems, in comparison, austerely classical, a poem in 12 books which is modelled closely on Virgil at every level from the architectural down to the details of the imagery and comparisons. But

Milton's very fidelity to Virgil makes more explicit the clash between Virgil's pagan world-view and Milton's Christian perspective. Like the *Aeneid*, the first two books of *Paradise Lost* feature a refugee hero who goes to the underworld, has love affairs, and founds a great nation; and yet that hero is Satan, who ought to be an incarnation of all that is evil. Thus, as well as conforming to the conventions of epic, Milton's poem throws out a series of challenges to them: how can you have an epic hero who is evil? What does that say about Milton's attitude to the form in which he is writing? Or does it indicate that Milton is really sympathetic towards the devil? As the poem continues, other candidates for the role of epic hero emerge: Adam has some of the required characteristics, but by no means all; Christ has some of them, too, except that his main achievement will be not to defeat his foes in battle but to allow himself to be killed by them. The poem in which this tension emerges is filled with imitations of Virgil, even down to the choice of individual words and word order. The paradox for Milton is that an epic narrative, in which a hero conquers his nation's enemies by force of arms, sits uneasily with a Christian world-view in which the ultimate act of heroism is Christ's action in allowing himself to be killed to redeem the sins of others. Milton's concept of a Christian epic, in which 'heroic patience', not military victory, is the ultimate prize, leads to a poem which is both a loving imitation of and in some ways almost a parody of Virgil.

One other related form deserves brief mention here: the 'epyllion', or little epic, a form developed in antiquity and very fashionable in late Elizabethan England. The epyllion was a narrative poem, typically on an erotic theme, with a grand style calculatedly close to self-parody, and often sexually frank in a style which would now be identified as pornographic. The best-known examples are Shakespeare's *Venus and Adonis*; Marlowe's *Hero and Leander*; and Thomas Nashe's *The Choice of Valentines*, a lurid and hilarious tale of sexual misadventure which prompted its twentieth-century editors to comment, 'There can, I fear, be little doubt that this poem is the work of Nashe' (Nashe, 1958, 5.141).

Satire

Satire is poetry written as criticism of the absurdity of the contemporary world. In some ways, satire is the natural opposite of pastoral: while pastoral is set in the countryside, the city is the natural habitat of the satirist; while pastoral is set in a timeless world, satire is acutely aware of the world today, of current fashions and current follies; while pastoral tends to see the world as fundamentally beautiful, satire tends to dwell upon the ugliness of the world, and the depravity of the human beings who live in it. As an example of satire which illustrates all three of these tendencies, one might take Ben Jonson's poem *On the Famous Voyage*. In it, Jonson describes an expedition by rowing boat up the Fleet Ditch, an enormous open sewer running along the edge of the City of London, which takes the adventurers past privies and workshops and piles of rubbish. At one point, the Fleet Ditch runs parallel to a street lined with bakeries and cooks' shops, so that, while the shops open onto the street, their back ends open onto the sewer:

> The sinks ran grease, and hair of measled [*spotty*] hogs,
> The heads, hocks [*leg-bones*], entrails, and the hides of dogs;
> For, to say truth, what scullion is so nasty
> To put the skins and offal in a pasty?
> Cats there lay diverse [*variously*] had been flayed and roasted
> And after mouldy grown, again were toasted,
> Then selling not, a dish was ta'en [*taken*] to mince them,
> But still, it seems, the rankness did convince 'em [*overcome them*].
> For here they were thrown in wi' the melted pewter,
> Yet drowned they not. They had five lives in future.
> (Jonson, 1925–52, 8.84–9)

Jonson's adventurers meet with a scene which is at once an exposé of contemporary fast food, and an opportunity for surreal flights of fancy on the part of the satirist. Much of the art of reading satire lies in detecting the changes of tone of voice. In this passage, Jonson's implication that those who make pies from dogs use only prime cuts of dogmeat in doing so is clearly sarcastic: the point is that no one ought to make pies out of dogs, even though they plainly do so. As for the indestructible cats, Jonson's tone here is an example of hyperbole, that is, overstatement for comic effect.

Renaissance satire such as Jonson's poem can be thought about in terms of two broad critical labels, 'Horatian' and 'Juvenalian', themselves derived from the names of the two best-known exponents of satire in the classical world, Horace and Juvenal. As a generalization, Horace's satires are gentle, ironic explorations of the folly of everyday life, written from a position of detached amusement. In Juvenalian satire, by contrast, the speaker is consumed with 'savage indignation' at the wickedness of the world. Where Horatian satire might offer suggestions for the improvement, or at least for the better toleration, of the world in which one finds oneself, Juvenalian satire tends to respond with rage and despair. One of the major critical debates about satire in the Renaissance period, and afterwards, is whether it is genuinely a reforming force aiming to make the world a better place, an idea which is more in tune with the Horatian ideal of satire, or whether, in fact, it is half in love with the vices it satirizes, and unable to think of any constructive alternatives to them: a model of satire more akin to that of Juvenal. As with the other types of poem discussed in this section, lyric, pastoral and epic, satirical poems repay thinking about not merely in terms of what they say, but in terms of how they relate to other poems within their genre.

DRAMA

Morality plays

The earliest form of drama with which we need to be concerned here is morality plays. Sponsored by the Church, these were designed principally as vehicles for the peddling of the official Church line, and they were, as their name suggests, primarily centred on moral issues and choices. Characters are secondary in importance to the exploration of these issues, and so are largely schematic and one-dimensional, with names which express their dominant role or qualities such as 'Good Deeds' or 'Kindness', while the hero is a bland, neutral figure like Everyman, hero of the play of that name. The action too is usually simple: the hero is tempted to sin by a tempter figure known as the Vice. He initially succumbs but finally sees the error of his ways and finds the path to salvation, while the Vice is exposed and disgraced.

It is with the Vice that a note of complication and subtlety enters this generally simple schema. The Vice was the one role in a morality play whose actor was not normally required to play more than one part (or if he was, the other part required of the actor was always very small) and was therefore given to the most accomplished performer in the company. The Vice's prominence was also confirmed by an important element in the structure of the performance of a morality play. Morality plays belong to the late fifteenth and early sixteenth centuries, well before any permanent theatres had been constructed in England (the first, the theatre on London's Bankside, was not built until 1576). Consequently these plays were acted in a variety of locations including inn yards and the halls of great houses and colleges, and it was the Vice himself who collected payment from spectators. It was thus possible to see the first part of the play for free; members of the audience were required to pay only if they wanted to stay long enough to see the antics of the Vice, with the odd result that you could be virtuous for free, but had to pay to be exposed to temptation and corruption. This amounted to an open admission that it was the wicked character who was the most dynamic and compelling in the play, and it is certainly the case that it is usually the Vice who initiates and dominates the action.

Morality plays fell out of favour well before the Renaissance period, but they did leave two major legacies.

The first is the prominence of the charismatic villain in so much Elizabethan and Jacobean drama: Marlowe's *The Jew of Malta* and Shakespeare's *Richard III* offer two obvious examples, and in *1 Henry IV* Shakespeare's Falstaff is openly compared to a Vice. The second is the strongly developed structure of morality plays, which sees the hero caught between a wicked character who tempts him and a good one who counsels him to virtue. This will be echoed many times in later plays, most notably in Marlowe's *Doctor Faustus*, where the hero is pulled in different directions by the bad advice of Mephostophilis and the good advice of the Old Man. The traditional staging of such temptation scenes, with the bad angel on one side of the hero and the good angel on the other, is also provocatively evoked in Kenneth Branagh's interpretation of Shakespeare's *Henry V*, where the Archbishop of Canterbury pours his war-mongering counsel into the king's ear. One final legacy of morality staging should also be noted: not only does the evil angel stand stage-left of the hero, but the left side of the stage in general is marked as both literally and metaphorically sinister ('sinister' means 'left' in Latin) and evil, and in some plays there is even a physical property placed there to represent the mark of hell, something which is remembered in Renaissance drama even as late as the 1590s play *Arden of Faversham*, where a character refers to it.

Tragedy

Arden of Faversham is one of the small but significant body of plays known as domestic tragedies, which collectively serve as a useful reminder that there is more to Renaissance tragedy than the familiar Shakespearean model. In fact, Renaissance tragedy is a complex and dynamic form which evolved considerably over the 50 or so years in which it flourished.

Tragedy as a genre originated with the ancient Greeks (the name probably derives from 'goatsong', and relates to the therapeutic, quasi-ritual functioning of the tragic hero as a scapegoat), and the rules of tragedy were codified by the Greek philosopher Aristotle in his *Poetics*. He said that the tragic hero should be a man who was generally good, and above the common run of mankind, but subject to a fatal flaw, or *hamartia* (in Greek this means 'failing to take aim correctly'). The story of this hero should pivot on a *peripeteia*, or reversal of fortune, and result in an *anagnorisis*, a moment of recognition when he, or she in the cases, for instance, of Medea and Antigone, realizes the precise nature of his or her mistake. As a result of this, the audience will ultimately be left with a feeling of *catharsis*, meaning the purging of the emotions of pity and fear. In addition, a tragedy must observe the three unities of time, place and action – that is, all the events must take place within 24 hours, everything must occur in the same location, and there must be no sub-plot. Although Renaissance drama does not always follow all of these rules – and, indeed, although most of it knows them only at second-hand through Latin scholars influenced by Aristotle – it never forgets their existence entirely.

It is reasonable to begin any survey of Renaissance tragedy with Christopher Marlowe's *Tamburlaine the Great* (1587). This simultaneously acknowledged and demolished the prevailing, largely medieval idea of tragedy as being the story of the fall of a great man, often attributable to nothing more than the inevitable turn of 'the wheel of Fortune'. (This pattern, most notably popularized in the collection of cautionary tales *The Mirror for Magistrates* [1574–87], is known as '*de casibus*', Latin for 'about falls'.) Marlowe's Tamburlaine is by no means unarguably a great man – though certainly a very successful one – and he spectacularly fails to fall. In fact the first of the two plays Marlowe wrote about him ends, like a comedy, with his marriage, and though he does die in the second, this may well have been an afterthought, the result of the first play's spectacular success, rather than an integral part of Marlowe's design. The play also introduced blank verse – unrhymed iambic pentameter – to the public theatre, and thus created the dominant voice of the great half-century which was to follow.

Marlowe continued to experiment with tragedy in *Doctor Faustus* (almost certainly written in 1588), *The Jew of Malta* (probably 1589), *The Massacre at Paris* (1590/1) and *Edward II* (1592), as well as the presumably early and possibly collaborative (with Thomas Nashe) *Dido, Queen of Carthage*. Perhaps the most striking thing about these bold and innovative plays is the extraordinary range of characters whom Marlowe chooses as his central figures: a Jew; an African queen; a homosexual English king; a damned black magicia; and a Scythian (regarded as one of the most barbarous of races). Equally clear is how broadly Marlowe interprets the idea of tragedy: as has already been noted, the first part of *Tamburlaine* ends more like a comedy, while *Edward II* and *The Massacre at Paris* are both as much history plays as tragedies (this is a generic overlap which will be visible throughout the period).

Marlowe's career was prematurely cut short in 1593 by his death, at the age of 29, in a stabbing in Deptford. Marlowe's fellow tragedian Thomas Kyd had also been snared in the intrigues that led to his death. Kyd, author of *The Spanish Tragedy*, was interrogated and tortured in connection with the events that led to Marlowe's arrest and death, and died the following year, possibly as a result of the tortures. Kyd's *The Spanish Tragedy* had been Marlowe's only serious rival for the domination of the tragic form in the 1580s. Elaborately rhetorical, it is heavily indebted to the Latin dramas of Seneca, which are usually thought to have been 'closet dramas' (that is, designed to be read rather than acted). It is distinguished by long, highly patterned speeches which soon came to appear old-fashioned. Kyd is also generally credited with having written a play on the story of Hamlet, known as the *ur*-Hamlet (from the German 'ur', original), but it is now lost, and it is not certain that he wrote it.

After the virtually simultaneous disappearance of Marlowe and Kyd from the scene, Shakespeare emerged into dominance in the 1590s and the first part of the 1600s. Shakespeare's earliest tragedies, *Titus Andronicus* and *Romeo and Juliet*, make considerable use of rhyming couplets, unlike his later plays which are much freer in this respect, and *Titus Andronicus* is also heavily Senecan in its indiscriminate piling-up of bloodshed and horrors. In this early period of his career Shakespeare also followed Marlowe in writing plays which can equally well be classified as tragedy or as history, most notably *Richard II* and *Julius Caesar*. But not until *Hamlet*, in the first years of the new century, does Shakespeare start to produce the kind of plays which now form our dominant image of Renaissance tragedy.

A number of possible factors may have influenced *Hamlet*. Some critics relate it to the early death of Shakespeare's only son, Hamnet. Equally, though, it can be clearly seen as affected by the two dominant political factors at the time of its composition: the unsuccessful rebellion of Queen Elizabeth's favourite, the Earl of Essex, in 1601, and the increasing certainty that when Elizabeth herself died (as she finally did in March 1603), her successor would be her cousin James VI of Scotland, whose life has often been seen as being echoed in *Hamlet* (for instance, James's wife was Anna of Denmark, and his stepfather, the Earl of Bothwell, died in Helsingor Castle, the model for Shakespeare's Elsinore).

Whatever its role in the shaping of *Hamlet*, the accession of James certainly brought about a marked shift in the tone of tragedy in general. The new king had barely come south from Edinburgh before John Marston produced his satirical tragicomedy, *The Malcontent*, which not only inaugurated a new genre but struck a new note of bitter, clever, cynical disillusionment with what came increasingly to be perceived as a corrupt court. 'O let my son fly the courts of princes,' says the virtuous Antonio in Webster's 1613 tragedy *The Duchess of Malfi*, and this is overwhelmingly the dominant note in the tragedies of the Jacobean period, which are also predominantly satirical in tone.

It is from these early years of James's reign that the rest of Shakespeare's major tragedies date. *Macbeth*, clearly written with an eye to James's Scottish ancestry and his known interest in witchcraft, *Othello* and *King Lear* had all been staged by 1606; *Coriolanus* and *Antony and Cleopatra* followed shortly afterwards. Nor did Shakespeare continue to have the field to himself. His friend Ben Jonson was writing tragedies based on Roman history from early in the 1600s, though they never matched the popularity of Jonson's comedies; George Chapman, Marlowe's friend, produced two tragedies based on French history; and, most notably, John Webster's two great tragedies, *The White Devil* and *The Duchess of Malfi*, appeared in 1612 and 1613 respectively. The first of these was a flop when it was first produced, as Webster bitterly records in the preface to it, but the second did much better and helped to establish the dominant note of Jacobean tragedy as increasingly dark and bitter. No one responded better to this than Thomas Middleton, whose major tragedies, *The Changeling* (co-authored with William Rowley) and *Women Beware Women*, both register the devastating effect of the Thomas Overbury scandal (see pp. 10–11), as does his tragicomedy *The Witch*.

Middleton's collaborator in *The Changeling*, Rowley, also collaborated on *The Witch of Edmonton*, with Thomas Dekker and John Ford. This was a late contribution to the genre of domestic tragedy, of which the two most notable were the anonymous *Arden of Faversham* (1590s) and Thomas Heywood's *A Woman Killed with Kindness* (1603). Domestic tragedy differs from 'tragedy of state' principally in centring on the small local doings of a particular household or households as opposed to those of a whole nation. To some extent this was an artificial distinction, because the idea of a close correspondence between the microcosm and the macrocosm meant that even the smallest household could be conceived of as representing the state in miniature. Nevertheless, domestic tragedies differ from tragedies of state not only in that the victim is merely a private householder rather than a ruler, but also in that domestic tragedies were almost always based on real-life recent crimes. *Arden of Faversham* is an important exception because the events it depicts, though historically accurate, were not recent; they were, however, sufficiently striking to make this the only non-royal story to appear in Raphael Holinshed's *Chronicles of England, Scotland, and Ireland*, illustrating the point that domestic tragedies were of wider and more long-lasting interest than might have been expected due to their local and particular origins. One result of this topicality is that, to ensure that they appeared swiftly, many domestic tragedies were parcelled out to multiple authors, and many were so ephemeral that all trace of them has now disappeared.

The Witch of Edmonton is a late example of the domestic tragedy genre, but also an early work of an author who was to become one of the most important tragic voices of the Jacobean and Caroline period, John Ford. Along with James Shirley, Ford was to take tragedy through almost to the closing of the theatres in 1642. A word often applied to the tragedy of this period is 'decadent': Ford's most famous play *'Tis Pity She's a Whore*, for instance, focuses on brother–sister incest, while his lesser-known but very powerful *Perkin Warbeck* focuses on an extremely convincing impostor, and the great tragedy *The Broken Heart* examines a group of people who feel driven to destroy themselves and each other in order to maintain their rigorous image of themselves.

Comedy

Early Tudor comedies, such as *Ralph Roister Doister* and *Gammer Gurton's Needle*, owe a good deal to the relatively unsophisticated traditions of morality plays, and would be unlikely to seem funny now. They are followed by the elaborate and highly rhetorical court comedies of John Lyly, such as *Midas* and *Gallathea*, and the laboured and loosely plotted ones of Robert Greene (e.g. *Friar Bacon and Friar Bungay*) and George Peele (e.g. *The Old Wives' Tale*). It is not until the era of Shakespeare and Jonson that we reach anything that would be really recognizable as successful comedy in our own terms.

Before considering Shakespeare's comedies, it is necessary to consider those of Jonson, his friend and chief rival. Students are most likely to come across one of Jonson's four masterpieces: *Volpone*, in which a bored old man amuses himself by pretending that he is about to die, in order to have people fawn on him in the hope of benefiting in his will; *The Alchemist*, a fast-moving farce discussed above in Chapter 1 in connection with alchemy; *Epicoene*, in which a man with a morbid fear of noise unwisely decides to find a woman to marry; or *Bartholomew Fair*, in which the great annual fair of London becomes the setting for a comedy revolving around marriage and trickery. An early Jonson play, *Every Man Out of His Humour*, advances a theory of 'humours comedy'; in such comedy, every character has one particular trait that makes them stand out from the others, often in the form of a strange and unreasonable obsession and/or a particular catchphrase. That trait, Jonson states, could be described as their 'humour', a pseudo-scientific word referring across to contemporary medical theory in which the character and actions of man are influenced by the chemical composition of the 'humours' which make up his body (discussed above in Chapter 1). The action of the comedy consists in setting these humorous characters in motion as if in a scientific experiment: watching their obsessions interact and conflict; and arranging a catastrophe, or conclusion, to the play, often involving the most humorous characters being humiliated or otherwise cured of their humour. Jonson's model is attractively clear, and can serve as a way of analysing not just Jonson's own comedies but also those of his contemporaries: for instance, *Twelfth Night* could be read as a series of humorous characters – Orsino with his unreasonable obsession with the idea of being in love, Olivia with her compulsion to be in mourning, Malvolio with his desire for social status – set into conflict and eventual resolution. The problem with it as a model is that it is somewhat reductive, implying, for instance, that all there is to *Volpone* (or to *Twelfth Night*) is a series of one-dimensional stereotypes, when in fact we might consider some of these characters more complex and nuanced than the theory advanced in Jonson's early plays would suggest. Additionally, the usual focus on Jonson's 'middle comedies' obscures the other riches of the Jonson canon: surreal and satirical early plays; two magnificent tragedies (*Sejanus* and *Catiline*); and a series of late plays, sometimes referred to dismissively as Jonson's 'dotages', which have in recent years increasingly been seen as analogues to Shakespeare's own late plays, still working, usually within the style of social comedy set in realistic British locations, but preoccupied with themes of reconciliation and renewal. But to consider these is to jump ahead chronologically, and we return now to the comedies of Shakespeare.

The plays of the early part of Shakespeare's career, up until about 1600, are almost entirely comedies and histories. What seem to have been the two earliest, *The Comedy of Errors* and *The Two Gentlemen of Verona*, encapsulate the patterns and motifs which will dominate his later plays. *The Comedy of Errors*, based on a play by the Roman dramatist Plautus, tells the story of two sets of identical twins, while *The Two Gentlemen of Verona* has a heroine who disguises herself as a boy in order to follow her absent lover. Confusion and disguises, especially in the shape of girls dressing up as boys, are staples of Shakespearean comedy. This is not just for the sake of generating comic misunderstandings, but also because such plot structures allow Shakespeare to explore serious issues of identity, social roles and the one-sex model (see p. 38–9). Whatever threat this may seem to pose to the social order is only temporary, however, since Shakespeare's comedies all end with at least one (and usually more) marriage. Normality is restored in other ways too: at the end of *Twelfth Night*, the respite afforded by the topsy-turvy customs of the holiday season comes to a close and Malvolio is released and restored to his position; at the end of *A Midsummer Night's Dream* and *As You Like It*, all the city-dwellers return from the 'green world' in which they have found a temporary escape from the pressures of the strict roles imposed by life within the urban community.

Shakespeare himself seems to have come to find this formula too neat and simple, for in his later comedies he complicates it considerably. It is for this reason that *Measure for Measure*, *All's Well That Ends Well* and sometimes *Troilus and Cressida* are known variously as 'problem plays' or 'dark comedies'. In marked contrast with Shakespeare's earlier, more festive comedies, these plays feature endings which are either not happy at all (in the case of *Troilus and Cressida*) or only equivocally happy (*Measure for Measure* and *All's Well That*

Ends Well). They also display a pronounced cynicism about all human relations, especially sexual ones, particularly since two of them depend on the plot device of a bed-trick, in which a man who thinks he is sleeping with the woman of his dreams is actually fobbed off with another one without even noticing.

These dark, cynical plays are for Shakespeare a stepping stone from comedy to tragedy, but they are also closely related to the sophisticated, disillusioned tone which will characterize the comedy of the early part of the seventeenth century. The two dominant forms are the Jonsonian comedy of humours (see pp. 76–8) and the city comedy at which Thomas Middleton above all excelled, which more generally reflected the audience to itself; in accordance with Aristotelian precept, which dictated that the hero of a tragedy should be above the audience but the hero of a comedy should be more or less on a level with them, it drew its characters from the same middling, merchant class as made up the bulk of the occupants of the seats at the Globe and other Jacobean theatres. It was partly this push to relate to the audience's reality which made comedy a much more risky business than tragedy, and a number of comedies of this period, most notably Jonson and Nashe's now lost *Isle of Dogs*, landed their authors in prison when topical references were felt to be too near the knuckle.

Tragicomedy

As we have already seen in the case of Shakespeare's problem plays, a number of the plays of this period did not readily adhere to the three main genres of tragedy, comedy and history. Particularly notable in this respect were the plays of Francis Beaumont and John Fletcher, which were huge popular successes from *c*.1608 – indeed as late as the 1660s it was Beaumont and Fletcher, not Shakespeare, who were felt to have been the major dramatists of the period. Beaumont and Fletcher's most famous plays are *A King and No King*, *The Maid's Tragedy* and *Philaster* (all written between

1608 and 1610–11), though the term 'Beaumont and Fletcher' is generally applied to a number of plays which were in fact produced by Fletcher in conjunction with other collaborators after Beaumont's early death. Their dominant feature is that they are surprising, with plots marked by unexpected twists and turns and unpredictable denouements, and that they adhere to the formula for tragicomedy which Fletcher described thus: 'a tragi-comedy is not so called in respect of mirth and killing, but in respect it wants deaths, which is enough to make it no tragedy, yet brings some near it, which is enough to make it no comedy' (Beaumont and Fletcher, 1953, 242). They exerted a considerable influence on other drama, which is most notably visible in Shakespeare's last plays, *Cymbeline*, *The Winter's Tale*, *Pericles* and *The Tempest*. These are like the problem plays in being neither fully tragic nor fully comic, but they are very different in tone, marked not by cynicism but by magic and miracle, and by the promise of renewal in the recurrent plot motif of an aged and erring father redeemed by a daughter.

Masques

Related to tragicomedy, and certainly equally influential, is the unique art form of the Jacobean and Caroline (i.e. from the reign of Charles I) masque. Masques differ from plays in a number of crucial respects. Plays were put on by professional actors in purpose-built public theatres and could be seen by anyone who had the price of admission; masques were performed at court by lords and ladies of the court (often including James I's queen, Anne of Denmark, herself), and were attended only by those with the required social cachet. Moreover, masques, unlike plays, relied heavily on plots and scenery. The first public theatres were all outdoor affairs, with a large part of the auditorium completely open to the elements (you can get a good idea of this at the reconstructed Globe on Bankside, which sells specially designed plastic macs to keep off the inevitable rain); not until the development of smaller, indoor theatres, around 1608, did special effects of any sort become feasible. Masques, by contrast, were performed entirely indoors, and elaborate costumes and special effects were so much a part of their nature that tension developed between Inigo Jones, who was responsible for the visual effects, and Ben Jonson, who produced the script – a war that would have been entirely unimaginable in the public theatre, where visual effects were minimal. The difference was underlined still further when Jones effectively won the argument, and the visual triumphed over the verbal. The final difference was that whereas plays tended to be at least covertly critical of the establishment – to the extent that many major playwrights of the period found themselves in prison at one time or another – masques were in many cases almost slavishly adulatory and flattering of royal policy.

History

Virtually all of Shakespeare's early plays which were not comedies were histories, and this was also a genre in which a number of other playwrights worked. Central to the age's understanding of history was Sir Philip Sidney's distinction in the *Defence of Poetry* between history and poetry. According to Sidney, poetry was the nobler form because it was not limited to telling the truth, which he saw as always bound to be less uplifting and inspiring than flights of fancy could be. Hand in hand with this went an idea that history was never really history, in the sense of being purely about the past, but always potentially a way of talking about the present. Moreover, it was an unusually safe way, since a play could avoid the ever-present danger of censorship by seeming to be about events that were safely done and dusted, when it really had contemporary applications.

The result of this is that Renaissance history plays, which may seem dry and inaccessible to us, were among the most urgently contemporary and interesting to their audiences. This can be seen in the danger that could attend on the writing of history in this period. The prose writer

John Hayward lost his ears for the controversial way in which he retold the story of how Henry IV usurped Richard II's throne. Similarly, the Earl of Essex's steward paid Shakespeare's company, The King's Men, to put on a play about Richard II (probably but not certainly Shakespeare's) on the eve of the Earl's rebellion as a way of encouraging the London populace to imitate Henry IV's act of usurpation, which was staged in the play. Nor was the story of Richard II the only one which was potentially dangerous to its tellers. Fulke Greville burned his play on the subject of Antony and Cleopatra when he decided that it might be seen as relating to the Earl of Essex's fall (even though he had, in fact, written it before the Earl's rebellion), and Samuel Daniel got into trouble for precisely the same reason over his Roman play *Philotas*, which Daniel said that he had written before the fall of the Earl of Essex but which subsequently came to look dangerously like a commentary on it.

As these two last cases suggest, a particularly politically charged branch of the history play was the Roman play. Rome was felt to be specially connected to Britain because of the legend of the *translatio imperii*, which said that when the Trojan prince Aeneas fled from the fall of Troy he went to Rome, where his descendants settled, until his great-grandson Brutus migrated from Troy to the uninhabited island of Britain, which he named after himself ('Britain' being supposedly derived from 'Brutus'). Renaissance Englishmen thus liked to think of themselves as the cultural heirs of Troy and Rome, something which is reflected in the numerous plays which tell or touch on the story of Brutus, ranging from the anonymous *Locrine*, which focuses on Brutus' son, to Shakespeare's *Cymbeline*, whose hero Postumus is clearly a type of Aeneas. (*The Tempest*, too, has many echoes of Virgil's *Aeneid*, which told the story of Aeneas' flight from Troy to Rome.) Even after the sceptical historian Polydore Vergil had demonstrated the extreme improbability of the legend, the story of the *translatio imperii* retained its hold on the English Renaissance imagination, and was much drawn on by the Tudors, since it enabled them to capitalize on their Welsh ancestry (i.e. 'British', since the Welsh were regarded as the original inhabitants of Britain).

The story of the *translatio imperii* thus fuelled the applicability of plays set in the past to contemporary Britain. Shakespeare's *Coriolanus*, for all its Roman setting, can in many ways be more readily mapped onto contemporary events than any other of his tragedies, since it seems to echo directly the Midlands corn riots at the time when it was written. In the 1620s and 1630s the unpopularity of Charles I's Roman Catholic wife Henrietta Maria found ready expression in a number of plays about the Emperor Claudius and his family which covertly used 'Roman' as a code for 'Roman Catholic', and capitalized on the fact that both Charles and Claudius limped and stammered. Indeed, in a famous incident the censor Sir Henry Herbert advised the playwright Philip Massinger to rewrite a particularly politically sensitive play, *Believe As You List*, which dealt originally with the Portuguese pretender Dom Antonio, by setting it in ancient Rome, which would serve to mask and defuse its tensions without him having to change its plot. Roman plays thus offer, paradoxically, one of the clearest windows onto the Tudor and Stuart world.

PROSE

Fictional prose

The first and most important point to make about Renaissance prose fictions is that they are not novels. When we study a long prose narrative, our expectations are often conditioned by prose fictions that we have studied before, and for most of us now that list is likely to include a number of novels in the tradition which includes Jane Austen, Charles Dickens and George Eliot. In works in this tradition, we expect realistically drawn characters that we can feel as if we know, and we expect quite a detailed picture of the 'inner life' of those characters – what they think and feel, and how they interact with their social world. Of course, many novels – particularly modern ones – fail to fit this description at all, but it remains a powerful stereotype, particularly when it comes to studying novels: we expect to be able to talk about the characters, first and foremost, then about the themes, then about how realistic or otherwise the world and plot of the novel seem to us. By contrast, Renaissance prose fictions are more various and fantastical than we might expect. Characters in them often seem unreal or purely symbolic in the style of Bunyan's *The Pilgrim's Progress*; their behaviour may be inconsistent from episode to episode. Their dialogue seems impossibly ornate, and we sometimes seem to have little access to what they are thinking. But there are other centres of interest in Renaissance prose fiction, and other pleasures there for the reader. This survey will give tastes of three examples, which between them offer an introduction to Renaissance prose fiction more widely: John Lyly's *Euphues* (published in 1578), Sir Philip Sidney's *Arcadia* (1590) and Thomas Nashe's *The Unfortunate Traveller* (1594).

First, we shall look at Lyly's *Euphues*, which enjoyed great contemporary success, not because of its characters or its plot, but because of its prose style. The central character, Euphues (whose name literally means 'well-speaking'), is an eloquent young man from Greece, admired for his elegant speech, who uses that gift of persuasion to make friends with the rich young Italian Philautus (whose name literally means 'self-lover'). Euphues then uses his gift of persuasion to steal Philautus's beloved Lucilla, and, to add insult to injury, writes Philautus a letter chiding him for his foolishness:

> But thou canst blame me no more of folly in leaving thee to love Lucilla than thou mayest reprove him of foolishness that having a sparrow in his hand letteth her go to catch the pheasant; or him of unskilfulness that seeing the heron leaveth to level his shot at the stockdove; or that woman of coyness that having a dead rose in her bosom throweth it away to gather the fresh violet. Love knoweth no laws. Did not Jupiter transform himself into the shape of Amphitryo to embrace Alcmene? into the

form of a swan to enjoy Leda? into a bull to beguile Io? into a shower of gold to win Danaë?

(Lyly, 1578, 31)

Euphues' letter goes on and on in a long and erudite catalogue of other classical gods who behaved deviously in the cause of pursuing love affairs. It is, of course, possible to read this passage as revealing something of Euphues' rather unpleasant character, or of the dynamics of his friendship with the equally shallow Philautus (whom he figures, in these three comparisons, as a sparrow, a stockdove, that is to say, a pigeon and a dead rose). But what really impressed Lyly's contemporaries was the style of the prose itself. Euphues demonstrates a mastery of *copia*, the Renaissance term for the seemingly effortless multiplication of supporting examples, drawn from natural history and mythology. His style is also marked by the elaborate lists of parallels; the alliteration; and the string of rhetorical questions with which this passage closes. (A rhetorical question is a question which does not really expect an answer: Euphues is not asking Philautus for information about whether or not the god Jupiter ever disguised himself as the mortal Amphitryo, but rather he is making the statement that Jupiter did so and making it more emphatic by phrasing it as a question.) Within the narrative, Euphues' mastery of persuasion seems to enable him to do anything he wants.

In fact, as the narrative develops, we are shown the limitations of Euphues' power. Lucilla proves as faithless to Euphues as she was to Philautus, and she justifies her conduct to him in terms which are as stylish and eloquent as those found in one of Euphues' own speeches. All the rhetorical tricks which Euphues himself has previously used are reused, by Lucilla, to destroy what he thought he had achieved using them, and Euphues becomes disillusioned with the limits to what he can achieve with his powers of persuasion. After a reconciliation with Philautus, Euphues returns from Italy to his home in Athens and devotes himself to increasingly pious (and wordy) meditations on the state of the world.

And yet it was the style of *Euphues* that created a sensation. The writer Thomas Nashe remembered, '*Euphues* I read when I was a little ape in Cambridge, and I thought it was *ipse ille* [the real thing]' (Nashe, 1958, 1.319). The style developed by Lyly, and known from *Euphues* as 'Euphuism', was widely imitated, not just in prose, but in drama and poetry as well in the years after 1578. In a sense, the most vivid character in *Euphues* is the prose style itself.

Like *Euphues*, the *Arcadia* of Sir Philip Sidney, written in the years leading up to his death in 1586, became a byword for a whole literary style. In Sidney's case, an entire textbook, *The Arcadian Rhetoric*, was written not long after his death, using examples from Sidney's narrative to illustrate a whole theory of stylish writing and speaking. The *Arcadia* revolves around two young princes, Pyrocles and Musidorus, who on their wanderings through Greece in search of adventure fall in love with the daughters of Basilius, ruler of Arcadia. Basilius is taking, in effect, an extended holiday from his duties as King, and has hidden himself and his family away in the countryside in one of the remoter parts of his kingdom. In their first scene together, Pyrocles and Musidorus debate over whether to stay in Arcadia or to move on. An extract from the dialogue illustrates the sophistication with which these characters speak, and the extent to which their language reflects, not how people actually talk to one another, but how people might aspire to talk to one another:

> [Pyrocles], desirous by degrees to bring his friend to a gentler consideration of him, and beginning with two or three broken sighs, answered him to this purpose: 'Excellent Musidorus, in the praises you gave me in the beginning of your speech, I easily acknowledge the force of your goodwill unto me; for neither could you have thought so well of me if extremity of love had not something dazzled your eyes, nor could you have loved me so entirely if you had not been apt to make so great, though undeserved, judgement of me . . . And lord! dear cousin', said he, 'doth not the pleasantness of this place carry in itself sufficient reward for any time lost in it, or for any such danger

that might ensue? Do you not see how everything conspires together to make this place a heavenly dwelling? Do you not see the grass, how in colour they excel the emeralds, everyone striving to pass his fellow – and yet they are all kept in an equal height? And see you not the rest of all these beautiful flowers, each of which would require a man's wit to know, and his life to express?'

(Sidney, 1985, 13–14)

This is only a short extract from Pyrocles' long and beautifully modulated speech, which starts with an elaborate opening compliment to his interlocutor, and moves through a developing series of arguments for staying rather than going. There are some similarities to Lyly's Euphuism – the list of rhetorical questions, the balanced parallels – but also some differences: Lyly's speakers, with their rote-learned lists of mythological comparisons, sound rather mechanical in comparison to Sidney's fluid, intelligent style.

The two princes decide to stay in Arcadia for a while in order to woo the two young women, and Musidorus disguises himself as a shepherd, and Pyrocles chooses to disguise himself as an Amazon. Rather alarmingly, Pyrocles makes an extremely convincing woman, so convincing that even the narrative voice starts referring to him as 'she' – a plasticity in the concept of character that a 'realistic' novelist would find unacceptable. The princes attempt to pursue their love affairs through many complications, doubts and dangers, with frequent halts for tournaments and poetry competitions, in a landscape filled with shepherds and lovers which is heavily influenced by the traditions of both pastoral and romance.

Perhaps the most striking feature of the text, though, is the fact that it exists in two different versions. The first, the *Old Arcadia*, offers a complete narrative in five books in which Pyrocles and Musidorus win their loves but end up on trial for the supposed murder of Basilius, a situation only resolved by the comic discovery that Basilius was not dead, merely sleeping. The *New Arcadia*, departing from the same opening situation of the princes falling in love with the princesses, turns into a far darker and more tangled story involving rival princes, violent abductions, torture and war. By halfway through the third book, it is unclear how the story could ever become light-hearted again, and at this point the *New Arcadia* breaks off in mid-sentence in the middle of a fight scene. Sidney himself had gone off to the Netherlands to fight and, as it turned out, to die in the wars there.

Hence, the interesting thing about Sidney's *Arcadia* is that, while it has two seemingly incompatible stories within it, it does have one seemingly coherent 'Arcadian rhetoric'. Again, prose style seems as important as storyline. Stylish, beautifully written and frequently sardonic, Sidney's romance inspired a series of imitations, from Thomas Lodge's *Rosalynde* and Greene's *Pandosto* (of particular interest as the sources, respectively, of *As You Like It* and *The Winter's Tale*) to *The Countess of Pembroke's Urania*, written by Sidney's niece Mary Wroth, which particularly explores how such a romance world might look to its long-suffering female participants.

In some ways, our third example, Thomas Nashe's *The Unfortunate Traveller*, is another descendant of the *Arcadia*, since it too features inset poems, tournaments and mistaken identities. But Nashe fuses this courtly style with a much earthier tradition of jest-books – collections of short humorous stories, frequently featuring the humiliation of the powerful, which also influence prose of the period, including Thomas Deloney's *Jack of Newbury*. *Jack of Newbury* is a wholesome episodic tale of hard work and success, telling the adventures of its citizen hero as he rises in society through his honesty and shrewdness. The world of *The Unfortunate Traveller*, though, is much darker than Deloney's, and is emphatically not a world in which hard work and honesty will necessarily bring any rewards at all. *The Unfortunate Traveller* is set in a Europe torn by pointless wars, swept by horrific plagues, and remarkable mainly for the casual cruelty of people's dealings with one another. At one point Nashe's narrator-hero Jack finds himself in Rome, sold as a slave to a wicked Jewish doctor who intends to use him as an anatomy demonstration: in other words, to cut him into pieces, while still alive, in front of an invited audience of medical experts. Jack passes an uneasy night in his cell:

> O, the cold sweating cares which I conceived after I knew I should be cut like a French summer-doublet. Methought already the blood began to gush out at my nose: if a flea on the arm had but bit me, I deemed the instrument had pricked me. Well, well, I may scoff at a shrewd turn but there's no such ready way to make a man a true Christian as to persuade himself that he is taken up for an anatomy. I'll depose I prayed then more than I did in seven year before. Not a drop of sweat trickled down my breast and my sides but I dreamed it was a smooth-edged razor tenderly slicing down my breast and my sides . . . in the night I dreamed of nothing but phlebotomy, bloody fluxes, incarnatives, running ulcers.
>
> (Nashe, 1958, 2.305)

This extract shows both the similarities and the differences between Nashe's style and those of Lyly and Sidney. Nashe's Jack is a colloquial narrator, whose speech is full of inter-jections such as 'O' and 'Well'; his is a calculated juxtaposi-tion of outrageous, amusing similes ('cut like a French summer-doublet') with a calculated simplicity to heighten the horror ('Methought already the blood began to gush out at my nose'). The last sentence in the extract, detailing what Jack dreamed of, and milking each word in the list for its sound and rhythm as well as for its shocking content, is typical of Nashe on top of his game. In *The Unfortunate Traveller*, the colloquial, joking style, at odds with the horrific (and surreal) subject matter, is at the centre of the work, just as Euphuism and the Arcadian rhetoric dominate Lyly's and Sidney's fictions respectively.

Non-fictional prose

Non-fictional prose literature, interestingly, also picks up on this concern with style. Thomas Dekker's *Plague Pamphlets* use many features of Nashe's style in trying to find a language to describe what happens when your home city is devastated by an outbreak of plague, as happened to London in 1603. Nashe's style was itself influenced by the Marprelate pamphlets, a set of illegally printed pamphlets written by an unknown Puritan author who went under the pseudonym 'Martin Marprelate' and attacked the corruption of the bishops. The resulting pamphlet illustrates an important feature of Renaissance non-fictional prose: it was frequently polemical, an act of persuasion like those dramatized by the unscrupulously persuasive Euphues. Edmund Spenser's *View of the Present State of Ireland*, circulated in manuscript in Spenser's lifetime and published 30 years after his death, is written to justify an English policy in Ireland which verged on the genocidal, and uses the form of a dialogue between two speakers in order to present its arguments more persuasively. Other wars of the period are frequently about religious matters, and Milton's prose pamphlets on the religious dimensions of divorce, church government and censorship are working within a polemical tradition partly defined by Marprelate and his ilk. But what unites the non-fictional and the fictional prose of the period is a concern with rhetoric, dialogue and persuasion: in short, with style itself.

LITERARY MOVEMENTS

Metaphysical poetry

Even though a group of poets including John Donne, George Herbert and Henry Vaughan are routinely described now as 'the metaphysical poets', the term 'metaphysical poetry' was not current in the Renaissance period, and the poets concerned were not consciously writing poetry of this kind. Rather, 'metaphysical poetry' is a retrospective label, first applied to Donne by another poet, John Dryden, in a piece of literary criticism written in 1693, more than 60 years after Donne's death: Donne, he said, affects the metaphysics, not only in his satires, but in his amorous verses, where nature only should reign; and perplexes the minds of the fair sex with nice speculations of philosophy, when he should engage their hearts, and entertain them with the softnesses of love.

(Gardner, 1957, 15)

As the *Oxford English Dictionary* documents, 'metaphysics' was defined by one Renaissance writer as 'things supernatural and the science of them'. Dryden, then, is complaining that Donne's poetry is too affectionately fond of academic ideas. It is worth noting that, while we might consider Dryden's observation a reasonable one, we might also object to the somewhat sexist implications of the rest of the sentence that 'the fair sex' (women) have minds incapable of ideas and should instead be interested only in the softnesses of love. Dryden is not exactly saying, 'Donne is too fond of thought rather than feeling, which is more important', but rather, 'Donne is too fond of thought, when the women he's addressing are only really capable of feeling'.

Be that as it may, the poetry of Donne, Herbert, and other metaphysical poets does share a recognizable style, characterized by the 'conceit', or extended comparison. Of this the most famous example is 'A Valediction Forbidding Mourning', in which a pair of separated lovers are compared to the twin legs of a pair of metal compasses.

If [our souls] be two, they are two so
As stiff twin compasses are two;
Thy soul, the fixed foot, makes no show
To move, but doth, if th'other do.

(Gardner, 1957, 74)

A pair of compasses consists of two metal rods joined with a hinge at one end. By putting one end on a fixed point on the map, and turning the other one around it, one can draw a circle. On the one hand, this image is incongruous: 'the softnesses of love', in Dryden's phrase, are being described by a simile from the hard-edged, unsentimental and unromantic world of navigation, trade and commerce. On the other hand, there is also a certain audacity in making as many points of comparison as possible between these two unlikely objects: one lover is travelling, the other is staying put, like the two legs of the compasses; yet they are connected; the fixed foot gives shape and meaning to the journey of the unfixed one – 'thy firmness makes my circle just'. The conceit, or extended comparison, is here used with virtuoso-like skill.

This means that metaphysical poetry presents something of a challenge to post-Romantic critics, who tend to value natural feeling over thought. In an essay published in 1921, T. S. Eliot described this separation of thought and feeling as the 'dissociation of sensibility', and championed Donne as a writer precisely because, it seemed to him, Donne celebrated the union of thought and feeling.

> A thought to Donne was an experience: it modified his sensibility . . . the ordinary man . . . falls in love, or reads Spinoza, and these two experiences have nothing to do with each other, or with the noise of the typewriter or the smell of cooking; in the mind of the poet these experiences are always forming new wholes.
>
> (Eliot, 1921, 669).

Again, Eliot's phrase 'dissociation of sensibility' is interesting, not just for what it reveals about Donne, but also for what it reveals about Eliot, with his vision of a society in which the ordinary man reads the philosophy of Spinoza, and houses are dominated by the sound of the typewriter and the smell of cooking. In some ways, this remark could be read as a comment on Eliot's own poetic mind, as much as on that of Donne. But it – and the essay from which it comes – provides a useful starting point and terminology for anyone looking at metaphysical poetry.

Women's writing

Just as metaphysical poets are studied as a coherent poetic movement although they did not much think of themselves us such, we study women's writing as if it were a distinct movement, even though women who chose to write were perhaps unlikely to be constantly thinking of themselves as part of a writing sisterhood. Having said that, one should add that one of the themes of much writing by women is the question of whether there is any point in a woman writing. For instance, in the course of a bitter pamphlet war between Thomas Nashe and Gabriel Harvey, an anonymous female writer weighed in on Harvey's side, expressing as she did so sarcastic doubts about whether she could compete with the vainglorious Nashe:

> Is't possible for puling wench to tame
> The furibundal champion of Fame?
> . . . Silly it is, that I can sing or say,
> And shall I venture such a blusterous fray?
>
> (Harvey, 1593, 2*4v)

The anonymous poetess, however, then enters into the slanging match with relish, calling Nashe a 'gag-toothed fop' and finishing with a couplet that presents herself as a female champion and Nashe as a maddened donkey:

> See how he brays and fumes at me, poor lass,
> That must immortalize the kill-cow ass.
>
> (Harvey, 1593, 2*4v)

The example of this writer shows that, although writing is often regarded as an indelicately masculine thing for a woman to be doing, it was not that women were incapable of entering into vigorous satirical exchanges. Joseph Swetnam's *Araignment of Lewd, Idel, Froward, and Unconstant Women* (1615) provoked a number of pamphlets in a similar vein, by writers including Rachel Speght, Esther Sowernam and Constantia

Munda, who argued that women were not necessarily lewd, idle, froward or inconstant, and that Swetnam's misogyny was unjustified and hypocritical. The last two of these three names are clearly pseudonyms, since Esther Sowernam's surname reverses Swetnam's (sour for sweet), and her first name is taken from a Biblical heroine, while Constantia Munda's name means, in Latin, 'pure constancy'. Nothing else is known about them or about the 'real' biological gender of the writers (as is also the case with Harvey's anonymous supporter). On the other hand, Rachel Speght is known to have written other works, and her life and marriage are attested in archival documents. So at least some of the contributions to the *querelle des femmes* – a useful term for the ongoing public debate throughout the Middle Ages and Renaissance about just how far women were inferior and subordinate to men – were themselves made by women.

Given the social pressure to remain modestly silent, few other female writers took part so directly and publicly in the *querelle des femmes*. However, something of that sense of pressure, of exclusion from public debate, can be felt in many other texts by women of this period, most of which take on less contentious forms, such as devotional writing or translation. The poet Martha Moulsworth, for instance, laments her lack of knowledge of Latin in a recently rediscovered meditative poem looking back on her life and three marriages (Moulsworth, 1993). The very few female-authored plays that survive are almost exclusively translations, such as Mary Sidney's *Antonie*, a translation from the French of a tragedy about Antony and Cleopatra which nevertheless holds a certain political charge simply by virtue of being a story about power and sex, or written for domestic, rather than public, performance (such as the work of Jane Cavendish and Elizabeth Brackley), or even not for performance at all. (This is the case with Elizabeth Cary's *Mariam*, a play designed to be read rather than performed.) It is in these domestic and private spaces that women's writing flourishes, but it is often profitable to think about it in terms of the spaces from which it is excluded.

Protestant poetics

On one level, the much-used term 'Protestant poetics' speaks for itself: it refers to the development of a poetic style appropriate to Protestant beliefs. Typical features of such a style are thought to include plainness of diction, personal introspection and application of scriptures to one's personal circumstances, although, as Young (2000) has pointed out, none of these features are strictly speaking unique to Protestant writing. 'Protestant poetics' works better, then, as a term referring to the stock of stories, metaphors and doctrinal positions characteristic of English Protestantism, of which Spenser's *The Faerie Queene* might serve as a good example. Typical Protestant tropes include a habitual comparison between Europe's oppressed Protestants and the Israelites oppressed by the Egyptians in the Old Testament, waiting for an opportunity to throw off their shackles; the figuration of the pope (or Rome as a whole) as the Whore of Babylon; and, more generally, an interest in the biblical book from which the image of the Whore of Babylon comes, the Book of Revelation (which also foretells the coming of the end of the world, and the entry of the godly into heaven). Spenser's *The Faerie Queene* is also characteristically Protestant in its repeated insistence that none of its heroes (or heroines) are capable of achieving their goals by themselves, just as no sinner is capable of redeeming his or her own sins without grace; all Spenser's heroes require the intervention of divine grace to help them complete their mission. The Redcross Knight of Spenser's *Faerie Queene*, Book I, is twice knocked out by the dragon he fights at the climax of the book, left apparently for dead, and surviving each time not because of his own merit but because of the life-giving grace of God. To this extent, 'Protestant poetics' is a term which can be as usefully applied to plot as to literary style.

The baroque

'Baroque' is a term with a broad range of meanings, covering Renaissance music, architecture and visual art as well as literature. Baroque emerges from the counter-reformation, that is, from the intellectual developments in Catholic Europe which occurred alongside the secession of parts of Northern Europe from the Catholic faith, and is an aesthetic which values ornamentation, often extreme ornamentation, rather than plainness, and also emotional intensity rather than restraint. It is best illustrated by an example, such as Richard Crashaw's *Hymn to Saint Teresa*, which describes in vivid pictorial detail the ecstatic religious experience of the Catholic Saint Teresa, an experience Teresa herself described as like being pierced with a spear. Crashaw imagines, in detail, each episode of the experience:

> How kindly will thy gentle heart
> Kiss the sweetly-killing dart!
> And close in his embraces keep
> Those delicious wounds, that weep
> Balsam to heal themselves with.

> (Ferguson, 1996, 425)

Crashaw's vivid and pictorial imagination of the scene, combined with the emotional lushness with which this moment of ecstasy is described, makes this a classic example of English baroque.

And yet, like Protestant poetics, the currency of the term beyond its most obvious examples is disputed. For instance, the baroque is characterized by intricacy and sometimes self-referentiality: is the play-within-a-play of Shakespeare's *Hamlet*, then, an example of baroque poetics? Donne's mannered style, brilliant paradox and intense emotion are all features of style associated with the baroque: and yet Donne has also been seen as exemplifying Protestant poetics, the supposedly opposed literary movement. Renaissance texts cannot, then, always be tidily assigned to one or another literary movement, but nonetheless the terminologies retain their usefulness: when analysing, for instance, the tragedies of Ford, baroque ideas of emotional force and pictorial intensity are very much to the fore.

3

Critical Approaches

Historical Overview
Key Issues and Debates

HISTORICAL OVERVIEW

It took a long time for study of Renaissance English literature
to gain the kind of widespread intellectual respectability it
enjoys today. Throughout the nineteenth century and even
into the twentieth, the hallmark of the truly civilized person
was thought to be not so much a knowledge of English literature, as a knowledge of Greek and Latin literature, and university degrees in English are a nineteenth-century invention.

As the study of English literature, and especially
Renaissance English literature, emerged from being the
interest of hobbyists into being at the centre of school and
university curricula, so the nature of discussion about that literature changed. Early critics were very much concerned
with distinguishing truly worthwhile literature from mere
dross, with Shakespeare often the chief focus of their attention and indeed veneration; in some ways, some modern
Shakespeare critics, such as Harold Bloom, follow in the lines
of this nineteenth-century school sometimes referred to as
belles lettres, in which the job of the critic is to point out the
aesthetic beauty of the literary object under discussion.

Another tendency emerging in the work of twentieth-
century critics was to read Renaissance literature both within

and as illustration of a historical context. This process, exemplified in E. M. W. Tillyard's classic *The Elizabethan World-Picture*, often tended to see Renaissance England as an ordered, hierarchical society, and its literature as a celebration of that order and hierarchy. Shakespeare's *Henry V* is a convenient test case for this approach, seeming as it does to offer a celebration of the British monarchy in the person of the charismatic Henry, who inspires his countrymen to a series of military victories over the French. For Tillyard, *Henry V* was a celebration of English and British valour, and one could characterize Olivier's 1944 film of the play – dedicated to the commandos then fighting in the Second World War – as a film incarnation of a Tillyard-like idea of the play.

And yet, as the wording of the above paragraph suggests, it is not hard to find problems and doubts in this reading of the play. For instance, Henry is an English king, and while he leads a group of soldiers including a Scot, a Welshman and an Irishman, his preparations for the war also include a discussion of the necessity of subduing Scotland lest 'the weasel Scot / Comes sneaking' to attack England from behind while he is in France (1.2.173–4). The play presents England as, at best, only uneasily in charge of Wales, Scotland and Ireland. Furthermore, Henry is an inspiring and effective war leader but, as has frequently been observed, the consequences for those around him are severe: he indirectly causes the death of several of his former drinking companions, he shows no mercy to personal friends who betray him, and his pursuit of the French throne culminates in a bloody battle which kills more than 10,000 people.

For a critic of the Tillyard school, convinced of Shakespeare's essential orthodoxy, this might be seen as just the necessary price of international justice and freedom. But if one does not share Tillyard's conviction that the Elizabethan state necessarily enjoyed the support of the people who made it up, another possible response is to argue that Shakespeare's intention in writing *Henry V* is to expose the dark underside of this idea of martial heroism, and to expose the psychological harm that the ideology of conquest inflicts on Henry himself, turning him from an ebullient youth into a soulless, Machiavellian war machine. From this view of the play arises Norman Rabkin's famous observation that the play is like a silhouette which could equally be seen as a rabbit or a duck – that is, that *Henry V* can be seen either as a celebration or a condemnation of Henry's imperialism, depending entirely on how it is looked at (Rabkin, 1977).

And yet a third twist in criticism of the play has been to move away from a reductive debate seeing the play in terms of Shakespeare's coded intention. This next step along this road is well represented by Stephen Greenblatt's essay, 'Invisible Bullets: Renaissance authority and its subversion, Henry IV and Henry V'. Greenblatt sees the literary text itself as to be read as an object of study in its own right, rather than as a simple way of accessing Shakespeare's own political opinion. For him, the most important political context of the play is the type of monarchy operating in Shakespeare's England, in which absolute power is established by Elizabeth's ability to display her wealth and influence, by inducing other people to display their subservience to her. Greenblatt is also influenced by Althusser's ideas of the power of the state, in which the state's ideology 'interpellates' its subjects – becomes fundamental and foundational to their sense of identity. Thus, concerning *Henry V* and the other history plays, Greenblatt writes:

> It is precisely because of the English form of absolutist theatricality that Shakespeare's drama, written for a theatre subject to State censorship, can be so relentlessly subversive: the form itself, as a primary expression of Renaissance power, contains the radical doubts it continually provokes . . . we are free to locate and pay homage to the plays' doubts only because they no longer threaten us. There is subversion, no end of subversion, only not for us.
>
> (Greenblatt, 1984, 45)

Greenblatt, then, argues that the text is both an expression of the power of the state, and yet at the same time, a resistance to it, since it includes the voices of characters (such as the Irish MacMorris) whom the play's conclusion ultimately represses. These voices threaten to 'subvert' the surface message of the play, to turn it from being a celebration to a condemnation. And yet, for Greenblatt, the very fact that the play can 'contain' these voices – let them speak and still let them be defeated – is a sign of the strength of the power of the state.

Much modern criticism continues to debate these terms of 'subversion' and 'containment', and raises the question of where and how literature, in all its forms, is political. Still, the closing sentence of Greenblatt's remark contains a shocking observation: as critics, we are still enmeshed within the state within which we write. We see the subversive potential of *Henry V* as regards the monarchy, because we no longer live in a monarchy of the type within which Shakespeare is writing. We like to find 'subversive' tendencies within the play, but only when they agree with what we already like to believe – when, in fact, they're no longer 'subversive' for us at all.

The case of *Henry V* can be considered as an example in miniature of a common process in the history of discussion of key issues and debates in the study of Renaissance literature: the three critics discussed here represent, in a sense, three phases of a debate which goes from treating literature as part and parcel of Renaissance orthodoxy, to treating it as a reaction against that orthodoxy, and on to a view in which literature can be reduced neither to celebration nor condemnation, but instead is a form which examines how that orthodoxy works. This three-stage process can be seen at work in some of the key issues that follow.

KEY ISSUES AND DEBATES

Gender and sexuality

We have already seen how a concept of a securely established gender identity, which may now seem fundamental to most people's concept of self, simply may not apply in the Renaissance because of the one-sex model, which suggested that gender was not something securely established but always in a state of flux. Nevertheless, women were treated differently from men. The position of women was precarious on every level. In *The Law's Resolution of Women's Rights* (1632), 'T. E.' wrote that all women 'are understood either married or to be married and their desires are subject to their husband' (T. E., 1632, 6). Legally, a married woman was a 'femme coverte', that is, her existence was 'covered', and indeed effectively subsumed, by that of her husband. The groundbreaking playwright and scientific figure Margaret Cavendish declared that she wrote her own autobiography 'lest after ages should mistake in not knowing I was daughter to one Master Lucas of St John's near Colchester in Essex, and second wife to the lord Marquis of Newcastle; for my Lord having had two wives, I might easily have been mistaken, especially if I should die and my Lord marry again' (Cavendish, 1656, 178). Even a woman who was a marchioness (and later a duchess), and a published author in her own right, feared to be forgotten or to be confused with someone else.

Not even Queen Elizabeth herself was immune to the suggestion of blurred identities. The biblical theory of types (see under 'Allegory' in the Glossary) was echoed in both the theory and the practice of Renaissance historiography, which was fond of detecting parallels between characters from history and contemporaries, especially rulers. This was graphically demonstrated when Elizabeth I could object to a play about Richard II with the words 'I am Richard II, know ye not that?': the implications of this in terms of the Essex rebellion are discussed above. Elizabeth's identification with Richard II also brings us back to the idea of the one-sex model, that men and women were not inherently different but potentially interchangeable. This is perhaps most interestingly illustrated in the closing scene of Shakespeare's *Twelfth Night*, where the twins Sebastian and Viola look exactly alike but are treated differently.

Ideas about sexuality appear to have been different too. The word 'homosexual' did not exist (it did not enter the English language until the 1890s) and it seems to have been assumed that rather than being exclusively attracted to one or other gender, most people – certainly most men – might find themselves attracted to members of either. Sexual behaviour which we would now class as homosexual was technically illegal, but in practice was likely to escape either comment or punishment so long as it was not accompanied by religious dissent, political subversion or too overt a challenge to the class system (the formula that is generally postulated is homosexual behaviour + dissent of any sort = sodomy, which was a crime punishable by death). Nowadays, we might well be likely to identify people as essentially either heterosexual or homosexual, but in the Renaissance period, perhaps we should not be looking for types of people but for types of behaviour. This has led to Lisa Jardine's provocative argument that when seventeenth-century moralists objected to men visiting theatres in which young boys appeared dressed as girls, their real fear was that the men would be attracted to the boys; hence, she argues, there is always a homoerotic flavour to Shakespeare's depiction of his heroines (Jardine, 1992).

Race

Another area in which Renaissance ideas of identity seem to have been different from ours is race. Now, the primary marker of racial difference – and something very loaded for us – is skin colour. However, those Renaissance explorers and traders who encountered people of non-white skin colours were not sure what to make of the fact. They did not know whether skin colour was a marker of ethnicity or a possibly temporary phenomenon produced by prolonged exposure to a hotter sun than they were used to in England. As Samuel Purchas wrote in *Purchas His Pilgrimage* (1613):

> Now if any would look that we should here in our discourse of
> the Negroes assign some cause of that their black colour: I

answer, that I cannot well answer this question, as being in itself difficult, and made more by the variety of answers, that others give hereunto. Some allege the heat of this Torrid Region, proceeding from the direct beams of the sun; and why then should all the West Indies which stretch from the one Tropic to the other have no other people? . . . why should Africa yield white people in Melinde? Some . . . attribute it to the dryness of the earth: . . . as though Niger were here dried up . . . Why then are the Portugals' children and generations white, or mulattos at most, that is, tawny, in St. Thomez and other places amongst them? Some ascribe it (as Herodotus) to the blackness of the parents' sperm or seed; And how made they the search to know the colour thereof, which if it hath (a thing by others denied), by what reason should it imprint this colour on the skin?

(Purchas, 1613, 545)

People in the seventeenth century could only theorize about what would happen if white people lived for a long time in Africa, or if black and white people intermarried. One of the colonists who encountered Native Americans in Virginia declared that 'their skin is tawny, not so born, but with dyeing and painting themselves', while John Smith of Pocahontas fame wrote in his *Map of Virginia* that the Native Americans were born white and only turned brown later (Price, 2004, 12). William Strachey, on whose report from Bermuda Shakespeare based *The Tempest*, also recorded that

They are generally of a colour brown, or rather tawny, which the mothers cast them into with a kind of arsenic-stone (like red patise, or orpiment) or rather with red tempered ointments of earth, and the juice of certain scrused roots, so soon as they are born, and this they do (keeping themselves still so smudged and besmeared) either for the custom of the country, or the better to defend them (since they go most what naked).

(Strachey, 1953, 70)

Along similar lines, the English writer Sir Kenelm Digby told a story of an 'Ethiopian queen who gave birth to a white child because a picture of the blessed Virgin hung over her bed' (Gilman, 2002, 120), while the Swedish writer Olaus Magnus speculated on whether the sperm of black men is black (Magnus, 1555, 3.1102).

Additionally, people in the Renaissance used the very words 'black' and 'white' in ways that were different from how we do. 'White' was not simply a descriptive word but a term of praise: the lady of the sonnet, for instance, was beautiful partly on account of her whiteness, and Renaissance Englishwomen were very careful to protect their complexions from any hint of the sun. Some even went so far as to whiten their faces artificially with lead powder (which we now know to have been poisonous). By contrast, 'black' connoted not only evil but also everything which was not white, and was a relative rather than an absolute term; when applied to people, it stretched to include not only those whom we would now call black but also those with dark hair or swarthy complexions (Callaghan, 1996). Hence when Shakespeare speaks of a 'Dark Lady' in his sonnets, he is almost certainly referring to a brunette rather than a black woman. On the one hand, this could lead to racism in quarters where we would not now expect to find it, most particularly against the Irish, but on the other it made for an attitude to other races which was, in some respects, perhaps more liberal than we might expect. For instance, when James VI/ I heard that the Englishman John Rolfe had married the Algonquian princess Pocahontas, he was initially angry – but only because Pocahontas, as the daughter of a king, was too good a match for Rolfe, rather than the other way around. Of course, it was important in this instance that Pocahontas had converted to Christianity and taken the Christian name Rebecca. To a Renaissance Englishman, she was therefore a perfectly acceptable bride, and indeed a Protestant Native American would almost certainly have been more acceptable to many Englishmen than a white Catholic would have been. Perhaps, finally, this is the strangest but most important idea for modern readers to accept: while the discourses of racial distinction were still in the formative stage, those of religious hatred and intolerance were already firmly established, and the distinction between Protestant and Catholic could sometimes be very nearly as loaded as the distinction between Christian and Muslim or black and white.

British studies

It is this emphasis on religion rather than race which explains why one particular group was always, in English eyes, literally and metaphorically beyond the pale. This was the Irish (the phrase 'beyond the pale' derives from the 'pale', or protective enclosure, which the English had established round Dublin to mark what they saw as the limits of civilization). A Moor like Othello might be exotic; a Scythian like Tamburlaine might be the hero of a play; but the real vitriol in Renaissance discussions of race is almost exclusively reserved for the Irish. Edmund Spenser, author of *The Faerie Queene*, served the English government in Ireland and wrote a devastating attack on its inhabitants in his *A View of the Present State of Ireland*, describing 'such customs of the Irish as seem offensive and repugnant to the good government of that Realm' (Spenser, 1633, 26). Spenser alleged that the Irish were not, as they claimed, descended from the Spanish, but from the Scythians, who were notorious among classical peoples as a byword for barbarity. For example, Shakespeare's King Lear, bitterly rejecting his daughter Cordelia, says she will henceforth be less welcome to him than even a 'barbarous Scythian' (1.1.116). Among the many instances of uncivilized behaviour which Spenser alleges against the Scythians, chief is the practice of what we now call transhumance, i.e. taking animals up onto higher pastures in the summer. This is a practice which aroused in Elizabethans a horror quite disproportionate to what it actually entailed: although it was simply good sense to move animals to where fresh grass could be found, Elizabethans interpreted it as evidence of a dangerously nomadic tendency in the people who practised it, and in some texts dark hints are dropped about men and animals

becoming too intimate in such circumstances. Using the
Irish term of 'bollying' for the practice, as if to mark the fact
that English had no word for it, Spenser alleges that 'by this
custom of bollying there grow in the mean time many great
enormities unto that commonwealth' (Spenser, 1633, 35).
Spenser also objects to the Irish habit of wearing a mantle
on the grounds that 'it is a fit house for an outlaw, a meet bed
for a rebel, and apt cloak for a thief . . . And surely for a bad
housewife it is no less convenient, for some of them that be
wandering women . . . it is half a wardrobe, for in summer
you shall find her arrayed commonly but in her smock and
mantle, to be more ready for her light services: in winter, and
in her travel, it is her cloak and safeguard and also a cover-
let for her lewd exercise' (Spenser, 1633, 37–8). He also
objects that the Irish 'draw the blood of the beast living . . .
to make meat thereof' (40) and that women have too much
power in Irish society.

In *A View of the Present State of Ireland*, Spenser's Irenius
declares that 'Scotland and Ireland are one and the same'
(Spenser, 1633, 27). However, the Welsh and Scots were generally viewed rather differently from the Irish, and also
differently from each other. The fact that the Tudors had
Welsh blood, and had many Welsh-born courtiers and
officials, made the Welsh seem much less alien than the Irish;
there may be some jokes about Welsh accents and their
alleged fondness for toasted cheese, but they are also seen as
the oldest inhabitants of the British Isles, through whom the
translatio imperii had been transmitted. The Scots were
regarded as different again. There was a long tradition of
hostilities between English and Scots on the border, where
the activities of Reivers (border clans who made virtually a
living out of stealing livestock and harassing their neighbours) on both sides gave rise to the term 'bereave', and after
James VI/I took the English throne in 1603 many of his
Scottish courtiers acquired an ugly reputation for grasping-
ness. Tensions rose so high that playwrights could find themselves in prison for making jokes about Scottish accents; one
of the reasons for publishing Spenser's *A View of the Present*

State of Ireland in 1633, so many years after it was written, may well have been its anti-Scots tone, because Charles I's decision that year to visit Scotland for a separate coronation ceremony there seems to have sparked off a wave of anti-Scottish feeling in London. The complicated and shifting relationship among English, Scots, Welsh and Irish has been the focus of much critical attention recently, with the emphasis on a new 'British history' which is much more willing than traditional historiography has been to recognize the conflicts and complexities within the British Isles, and has offered particularly interesting analyses of plays like *Henry V* and *Cymbeline*, which contain Welsh characters, and John Ford's late 'British' history play *Perkin Warbeck*, in which a Flemish-born pretender to the English throne lands first in Ireland and then in Cornwall after receiving aid from the king of Scotland.

Space and geographies

'New philosophy calls all in doubt', said John Donne and, of the various new branches of knowledge that he might have been thinking of, new ideas about space and geography were both some of the most exciting and some of the most threatening in the Renaissance period. On the one hand, Renaissance explorers were penetrating further into previously unexplored corners of the globe than ever before. Sir Francis Drake rounded South America and sailed up the other side as far as Vancouver Island; an Englishman, William Adams, was living in Japan; an English colony was successfully established in North America in 1607, afer an earlier abortive attempt in 1585; Englishmen were trading with Russia, India and Turkey, and Marlowe's Tamburlaine could imagine the idea of the Suez Canal hundreds of years before it was built. Undoubtedly these rapidly expanding horizons, and the exciting emergence of new protocols and projections for mapping them, energized English Renaissance literature, as seen in a wide variety of texts from Marlowe's *The Jew of Malta*, loosely based on the siege of Malta by the Turks in 1565, to

Shakespeare's *The Tempest*, inspired by a shipwreck off Bermuda in 1609, to Fletcher's *The Island Princess*, centred on Portuguese trading interests in the Spice Islands.

A number of these plays, though, reveal tensions as well as delight in the new possibilities. In the first place, the failure of the Bible to mention the New World cast doubt on the supposed omniscience of the Scriptures. As Strachey noted in *The Historie of Travell into Virginia Britania*,

> It were not perhaps too curious a thing to demand how these people might come first, and from whom, and whence, to inhabit these so far remote westerly parts of the world, having no intercourse with Africa, Asia nor Europe, and considering the whole world, so many years, (by all knowledge received, was supposed to be only contained and circumscribed in the discovered and travelled bounds of those three . . . as also to question how it should be, that they (if descended from the people of the first creation) should maintain so general and gross a defection from the true knowledge of God, with one kind, as it were of rude and savage life, customs, manners, and religion? it being to be granted, that with us (infallibly) they had one and the same descent and beginning from the universal deluge, in the scattering of Noah his children and nephews, with their families (as little colonies) some to one, some to other borders of the Earth to dwell?
>
> (Strachey, 1953, 53)

Secondly, the New World became all too often a site of religious and interracial tensions rather than an escape from them. The exploration of America in particular was conducted along religiously demarcated lines: William Strachey in *The Historie of Travell into Virginia Britania* spoke of how the Indians planned

> to break into our Plantations with acts of hostility (as most despitefully did Pedro Melendes, their Admiral, into the French colony 44 years since in *Nova Francia*, who razed their fort, and hung up the common Soldiers . . . and wrought over them

disdainful Inscriptions in Spanish, importing, *I do not this as unto Frenchmen, but as unto Lutherans.*

(Strachey, 1953, 16)

Most seriously, voyages of exploration repeatedly refused to yield the dividends which had been hoped for. One of the great aims of Renaissance exploration was to make the journey to the Far East, location of the highly profitable Spice Islands, easier by cutting either across the top of North America or across the top of Europe rather than having to go round by the Cape of Good Hope. But both the North-West Passage and the North-East Passage proved impossible to locate, and in the reign of Mary I an entire expedition led by Sir Hugh Willoughby was found frozen to death in the icy waters off Lapland. Samples of rock brought home from Virginia proved not to contain gold, and there were disquieting rumours of hunger, internal dissension and trouble with natives in the fledgling colony. Travel, then, represents troubled waters as well as excitement and possibility for English Renaissance literature.

Personal identity

Renaissance people were much more likely than we are to define their sense of self in terms of who they were related to. Before the introduction of parish registers in 1538, kinship was essentially remembered rather than recorded, and kinship was recognized at far greater removes than we would now be likely to do. In *A View of the Present State of Ireland*, Eudoxus declares that 'This ripping up [examination] of Ancestries is very pleasing unto me' (Spenser, 1633, 34), and this was a view that many Elizabethans would certainly have shared. The diarist John Manningham recognized as a relative the great-granddaughter of a relation of his cousin's first wife's sister's husband, while the Dowager Countess of Arundel spoke of the aunt and uncle of her daughter-in-law as her brother and sister. This was particularly the case when it came to using marriage alliances to claim kin with someone powerful: the politician Sir Giles Mompesson, for instance, built his career partly on the fact that his sister-in-law was married to the half-brother of the Duke of Buckingham, the favourite of James VI/I.

It is not appropriate, then, to simply map our own ideas of selfhood onto sixteenth- and seventeenth-century people. In particular, a word that has attracted much attention in writing on Renaissance literature over the last few years is 'subjectivity'. As Catherine Belsey puts it in her book *The Subject of Tragedy*,

> To be a subject is to have access to signifying practice, to iden-tify with the 'I' of utterance and the 'I' who speaks. The subject is held in place in a specific discourse, a specific knowledge, by the meanings available there. In so far as signifying practice always precedes the individual, is always learned, the subject is a subjected being, an effect of the meanings it seems to possess.
>
> (Belsey, 1985, 5)

Although Belsey concedes that 'there are in the plays of the late-sixteenth and early seventeenth centuries intimations of the construction of a place which notions of personal iden-tity were therefore to come to fill' (Belsey, 1985, 40), she argues that we should not see the characters of Renaissance literature (and particularly not the female characters) as fully unified and autonomous. 'Who is it that can tell me who I am?' asks Shakespeare's King Lear; for the Renaissance, identity was indeed always constituted by and dependent upon other people as well as on oneself.

Past and present

Should we try to read the past on its own terms, or might this interfere with our own response to texts? This is a question that has recently been the subject of much critical attention. Why, after all, should we study Renaissance literature at all if it is entirely bound up with its own time, which is now long since past? The debate is reflected in a significant shift in recent years from one dominant critical paradigm to another. For the last two decades of the twentieth century, New Historicism, a term coined by Stephen Greenblatt, led the way. This emphasized above all reading texts within their historical contexts. More recently, though, 'presentism' has emerged as a force, and this seeks to explore not what Renaissance drama *used* to mean but what it means *now*. As Terence Hawkes puts it in his defence of presentist criticism, with an ironic reference to the self-proclaimed desire of the most famous of New Historicists, Stephen Greenblatt, to 'speak with the dead', 'A Shakespearean criticism that takes [the present] on board will not yearn to speak with the dead. It will aim, in the end, to talk to the living' (Hawkes, 2002, 4). On the other hand, how can we read texts which were written 400 years ago in isolation from the circumstances which produced them? If we do so, we are in danger of coming out with apparently absurd statements such as Hawkes's that 'a fully paid-up presentist will always feel entitled to ask how the influence of Shakespeare on Marx or Freud matches up to the influence of Marx or Freud on Shakespeare' (Hawkes, 2002, 4). Hawkes, however, might well defend his position by contending that 'History is far too important to be left to scholars who believe themselves able to make contact with a past unshaped by their own concerns' (Hawkes, 2002, 3). This neatly makes the point that there is not actually any such thing as a 'history' to which we have unmediated access, and that it is too easy simply just to fall back on sets of 'facts' which we may think we know about the past.

Perhaps the most extreme form of the debate can be found in the polarized positions of historicists, who seek to situate Renaissance texts firmly in their historical and cultural contexts, and those who use psychoanalytic theory to read them. The influential New Historicist Stephen Greenblatt, for instance, wrote in an influential essay that although 'the universalist claims of psychoanalysis are unruffled by the indifference of the past to its categories', there are nevertheless important historical differences conditioning the construction of the self and that therefore 'the historical mode of selfhood that psychoanalysis has tried to universalize into the very form of the human condition' is a pernicious misrepresentation (Greenblatt, 1990, 136–7). Greenblatt contends, and many others have concurred with him, that the idea of individual identity is in many ways an essentially modern one; in the early modern period, he suggests, the self was conceived of much more as part of a material and social network.

However, there are also tensions between various different kinds of historicist critics. New Historicists (who tend to be US-based) typically put a famous Renaissance text alongside a much less well-known cultural artefact produced at roughly the same time and read the two together as equally representative of a culture. On the one hand, this may lead to a welcome breaking away from the constraints of the traditional canon, but on the other hand, one might also sometimes feel that the connections between the paired texts are rather loosely defined. Moreover, this can lead to fragmentation, as Jean E. Howard points out: 'recent historicist attention has often focused on moments in a text, rather than on its overall narrative structure . . . historicist reading practice often deliberately fractures a text, forcing the juxtaposition of certain of its elements with materials from the extraliterary world. To such critics, genre is uninteresting, because they primarily wish to connect literary texts not to other literary texts but to other *kinds* of texts in the larger field of cultural practices' (Howard, 2003, 302). Cultural Materialists (who are more likely to be UK-based) are more interested in the cultural uses to which Renaissance texts have been put in the recent past, as with Terence Hawkes' examination of a production of Shakespeare's *Coriolanus* at the time of the General Strike in 1926 (Hawkes, 1992).

The increasingly fashionable 'presentist' approach takes this a step further. Ben Jonson said that Shakespeare 'was not of an age, but for all time', and it is precisely in this apparent ability to transcend time that his greatness has often been felt to lie. It is certainly true that Shakespearean plays in production have often been made to speak very powerfully to contemporary concerns and situations (take, for example, the use of *Henry V* as propaganda in the 1944 Ministry of Defence-funded Olivier film and by Kenneth Branagh as a critique of war in his very different post-Falklands War film). Nor is Shakespeare the only writer who can speak to modern times in this way. In her essay 'Marlowe *in tempore belli*', Leah Marcus declares that 'many literary scholars have watched the unfolding of recent events in Afghanistan and Iraq with Marlowe on their minds', while Patrick Cheney, too, speaks of how Marlowe puts at the centre of his stage 'two cultural topics now absorbing the world, the fate of Jews and the role of Islam' (Marcus, 2004, 295; Cheney, 2004, 17). And in the 1980s the playwright Howard Barker adapted Middleton's tragedy *Women Beware Women* to make into it a commentary on the royal wedding of Charles and Diana.

On the other hand, there are many Renaissance texts which would be very hard indeed to make sense of without some grasp of their historical and cultural contexts. What, for instance, would we be able to make of *The Faerie Queene* if we had no understanding of allegory as a mode, or of the role of fairy mythology or imagery in the personal iconography of Elizabeth I, or of the Elizabethan military campaigns in Ireland? What sense would it make to read Shakespeare's *Richard II* without knowing that, to audiences of its own day, it seemed to relate to the Earl of Essex? When it comes to poetry, almost all of the religious verse of the period – a form in which some of the most talented writers of the time invested their greatest creative and emotional energies – would be entirely incomprehensible without a grasp of the religious tensions of the sixteenth and seventeenth centuries.

Particularly problematic is the case of texts that can make sense to us now but which would have made a very different sort of sense to their original readers and audiences. How, for instance, should we read *The Merchant of Venice* – as a play about anti-Semitism in terms of our post-Holocaust understanding of everything which that can lead to, or as the product of an age in which it might have seemed actually right and indeed positively benevolent and meritorious to force Shylock to convert to Christianity? Moreover, if we do choose the latter reading, can we ignore the parallels with some extreme branches of Islamic militancy today, which would similarly insist that non-believers must convert or die? Ironically, in this respect, the attempt to put Shakespeare back into his own culture seems only to make him speak more loudly to ours. But that may not always be the case with Renaissance texts. John Lyly's *Euphues* and William Warner's *Albion's England* were highly valued in their own day, and more recent scholarly work can help show why this was the case, but few students will be persuaded that these works are still urgent and important and interesting now. Tastes change, and these seem to be two examples of works that were indeed not for all time but of an age; should we, though, simply forget them on those grounds, or should we study them to help give us a fuller picture of that age? To us, while the many, various and rich works of Renaissance literature may indeed speak to the present, we could not envisage divorcing them from their original cultural and historical contexts. This book has aimed to give a flavour of some of those contexts, and of how they may be explored, and of how they may enrich our understanding of the literature of the Renaissance.

4

Resources for Independent Study

CHRONOLOGY OF KEY HISTORICAL AND CULTURAL EVENTS

1453 Fall of Constantinople to the Turks.

1455 Gutenberg Bible.

1485 Henry, Earl of Richmond, last claimant of the Lancastrian line, defeats the Yorkist king Richard III at the Battle of Bosworth and becomes the first king of the Tudor dynasty. He later marries the Yorkist heiress Elizabeth to unite the claims of the two houses and bring the Wars of the Roses to an end.

1492 Columbus discovers America.

1502 Death of Prince Arthur, elder son of Henry VII and first husband of Catherine of Aragon.

1509 Henry VII dies and is succeeded by his only surviving son, Henry VIII.
Henry VIII marries Catherine of Aragon.

1516 Mary Tudor born. Later to become Mary I, she will be the only surviving child of Henry VIII and Catherine of Aragon.

1517 Martin Luther nails his 95 theses to the door of the Castle Church in Wittenberg.

1528 Baldessare Castiglione, *The Book of the Courtier*, is published in Italy.

1533 Henry VIII marries Anne Boleyn after Archbishop Cranmer has declared his marriage to Catherine annulled and Henry has pronounced himself Supreme Governor of the Church of England.
The future Elizabeth I is born to Henry VIII and Anne Boleyn.

1536 Publication of Calvin's *Institutes of the Christian Religion* in Geneva.
Anne Boleyn is executed.
Henry VIII marries Jane Seymour.

1537 The future Edward VI is born to Henry VIII and Jane Seymour. Jane Seymour dies 12 days later.

1540 Henry VIII marries Anne of Cleves but the marriage is annulled six months later and Henry VIII marries Catherine Howard.

1542 Execution of Catherine Howard.
Death of the poet Sir Thomas Wyatt.
Death of James V of Scotland, nephew of Henry VIII. His week-old daughter Mary succeeds as Mary, Queen of Scots.

1543 Andreas Vesalius, *De Humani Corporis Fabrica* (*Of the Making of the Human Body*), is published in Italy.
Henry VIII marries Catherine Parr.

1547 Death of Henry VIII. His only son Edward succeeds as Edward VI.

1553 Death of Edward VI. After quelling a brief rising in favour of Lady Jane Grey, his elder sister Mary succeeds as Mary I and works to restore Catholicism.

1557 *Tottel's Miscellany* is published.

1558 Mary, Queen of Scots marries the Dauphin of France.
Death of Mary I. Her sister Elizabeth succeeds as Elizabeth I. Protestantism once more becomes the official religion.

1560 The 16-year-old Dauphin of France dies of an ear abcess.

1561 The widowed Mary, Queen of Scots returns to Scotland.

1564 Christopher Marlowe is christened.

William Shakespeare is christened.

1565 Siege of Malta by the Turks.

Mary, Queen of Scots marries her cousin Henry, Lord Darnley.

1566 The future James VI of Scotland and James I of England is born to Mary, Queen of Scots and Henry, Lord Darnley.

1567 Lord Darnley is murdered.

Mary, Queen of Scots marries James Hepburn, Earl of Bothwell, who was widely believed to have been responsible for the murder of Lord Darnley.

1568 Mary, Queen of Scots is defeated by rebel Scottish nobles at the Battle of Langside. She flees to England, where she will be kept captive for the next 19 years.

1570 Pope Pius V excommunicates Elizabeth I.

1571 The Turks are defeated at the battle of Lepanto, off the coast of Greece.

1576 Construction of The Theatre in London, the first purpose-built public playing space in England.

1585 Sir Richard Grenville establishes the first English colony in the New World, at Roanoke, off the North Carolina coast.

1586 Death of Sir Philip Sidney after being mortally wounded fighting the Spanish in the Netherlands.

1587 Christopher Marlowe's *Tamburlaine the Great* Parts One and Two are performed.

Execution of Mary, Queen of Scots.

1588 –90 Martin Marprelate pamphlets are published.

1588 The Spanish Armada is sighted in the Channel.

The Spanish Armada is routed.

1590 Publication of the first three books of Spenser's *The Faerie Queene* and of Sir Philip Sidney's *The Countess of Pembroke's Arcadia*.

1592 The domestic tragedy *Arden of Faversham* is printed.

1593 Death of Christopher Marlowe.

1594 Execution of the queen's Portuguese doctor Rodrigo Lopez for allegedly plotting to murder her.

1596 Books 4–6 of *The Faerie Queene* are published.

1598 Francis Meres' *Palladis Tamia* offers a snapshot of the London literary scene.

1599 The Globe Theatre is built. One of the earliest plays to be staged there is Shakespeare's *Henry V*, which contains a topical reference to the Irish wars then being conducted by the Earl of Essex.

1601 *Hamlet* and *Twelfth Night* first performed?
The Earl of Essex leads an abortive rebellion against Elizabeth I, for which he is beheaded.

1603 Death of Elizabeth I. James VI of Scotland succeeds as James VI/I.

1604 Publication of the A Text of *Doctor Faustus*. *Othello* first performed?

1605 Ben Jonson, *The Masque of Blackness* is performed. *Macbeth* is first performed?

1606 First recorded performance of *King Lear*.

1607 Food riots in the Midlands. Donne's *Divine Poems* is published.

1608 Public playing starts at the Blackfriars, the first indoor theatre in London.

1609 Wreck of the *Sea Venture* off Bermuda. This will provide the source for Shakespeare's *The Tempest*.
Shakespeare's sonnets are printed.

1610 Ben Jonson's *The Alchemist* is performed. *The Winter's Tale* is first performed?

1612 Webster, *The White Devil* is printed. Galileo, *The Discourse on Floating Bodies* is published.
Death of Henry Prince of Wales, eldest son of James VI/I.

1613 Webster, *The Duchess of Malfi* is performed?
Murder of Sir Thomas Overbury.

1616 Publication of the B Text of *Doctor Faustus*.

1616 Death of Shakespeare.

1622   Thomas Middleton and William Rowley, *The Changeling* is performed.

1623   First Folio of Shakespeare's plays.

1624   Thomas Middleton, *A Game at Chess* is performed.

1625   Death of James VI/I. His only surviving son Charles succeeds as Charles I.

1626   Charles I marries the French princess Henrietta Maria.

1628   Assassination of the Duke of Buckingham, favourite of first James I and then Charles I.

1629   Charles I suspends Parliament. It is not reconvened until 1640.

1633   Death of George Herbert and publication of his poems.

1634   John Milton's *Comus* is performed.

1642   Charles I raises his standard at Nottingham. The English Civil War begins.
The theatres are closed by order of Parliament. They will not reopen until the Restoration (1660).

1649   Execution of Charles I.

1660   Restoration of Charles II.

1667   Publication of the first version of John Milton's, *Paradise Lost*.

1678   Death of Andrew Marvell. His *Miscellaneous Poems* are printed three years later.

GLOSSARY OF KEY TERMS AND CONCEPTS

Allegory

Allegory essentially means a figure, narrative or image which is really alluding to something other than what it is purporting to describe; a particularly famous example is C. S. Lewis's *The Lion, the Witch and the Wardrobe*, which appears to be about a magic lion but is really about Jesus. The big question with allegory is always what it is *really* about, although in some cases there can be many levels of allegory, with each element of the text representing more than one thing simultaneously. Renaissance allegory can be traced back to the idea that there is a series of correspondences between characters in the Old Testament of the Bible and characters in the New Testament. Characters who are seen to be related in this way are called 'types' of each other. A good example is Jonah, who spent three days in the stomach of a whale before re-emerging and is therefore a 'type' of Christ, who was dead for three days and was then resurrected. The second major influence on Renaissance allegory was the popularity of 'emblem books', which printed pictures accompanied by verses which commented on their meaning; for instance, someone playing cards was an emblem of idleness, while a woman looking in a mirror was an emblem of vanity. These ideas of correspondence between one thing and another, often expressed in visual terms, lie behind Renaissance allegory. The most famous example of the genre is Edmund Spenser's *The Faerie Queene*, which represents (or 'figures') Elizabeth I in a variety of allegorical guises ranging from Titania, the fairy queen, to Britomart, the female warrior.

Blank verse

Blank verse consists of lines of unrhymed iambic pentameters (see Glossary entry). It was first developed in university drama, brought to the public stage by Marlowe, and rapidly became the standard metre for English drama and for some poetry too (e.g. *Paradise Lost*), partly because it was generally believed to offer the closest approximation to the natural rhythms of everyday speech.

Chorography

Literally 'the study of land', chorography, in the form of detailed descriptions in prose or poetry of particular locations, became a popular Renaissance genre. The most interesting example is Michael Drayton's *Poly-Olbion*, which offers minutely detailed, poetic surveys of the English landscape. (Drayton had hoped to cover Scotland too, but died before he could do so.)

Classical

The term 'classical' refers literally to the period of the dominance of ancient Greece and Rome. It was used with particular reference to the artistic forms produced by the two civilizations, most notably architecture, art and Greek and Latin literature.

Closet drama

Closet drama was drama written to be read rather than performed. The tragedies of the Roman author Seneca, which were hugely influential on the first wave of English Renaissance tragedy, were written as closet drama, and included horrific acts of violence which would have been difficult as well as disturbing to stage. The first Englishwoman to publish a play which she had written, Elizabeth Cary, wrote her *Tragedy of Mariam* (published 1613) as closet drama because it would have been disgraceful for a woman to write for the public stage.

Conceit

This is one of the most misleading terms used to describe Renaissance literature because we will be tempted to think it carries the same meaning as our modern word 'conceit', but in fact it is very different. A conceit for a Renaissance poet is the idea of linking two apparently dissimilar things and finding some form of parallel between them. For an example, see the discussion of Donne's poem 'A Valediction: Forbidding Mourning' (pp. 91–2 above).

Eclogue

A short poem, generally concerned with or set in the context of the pastoral, and often in the form of a dialogue, is called as eclogue. In Sidney's *The Countess of Pembroke's Arcadia*, the shepherds (and princes disguised as shepherds) stage singing contests in which they attempt to outdo each other in the singing of eclogues.

Epic

An epic is a long poem divided into either 12 or 24 books (Spenser's *The Faerie Queene* has only six, but that is because it was left unfinished; 12 books were originally projected). The great models for epic poems were the Greek *Iliad* and *Odyssey*, attributed to Homer (though now generally believed to be the work of many hands) and the Latin *Aeneid*, written by Virgil. An epic poem generally had a single hero, after whom it was often named (thus the *Odyssey* is the story of Odysseus and the *Aeneid* is the story of Aeneas), and often dealt with matters of national destiny. Because the writing of an epic is such a massive undertaking, the history of the Renaissance is littered with projected epic poems which were never begun or were left unfinished, as well as the few which were ultimately written, such as the epics on the subject of Macbeth or of King Arthur which Milton considered writing before finally settling on *Paradise Lost*.

Epic simile

This is a sustained comparison, often spanning several lines. In many cases the 'vehicle' (thing used as a point of comparison) is brought so vividly to life that we may almost lose sight of the 'tenor' (thing being described). Nonetheless, the pleasure of an epic simile lies in discerning multiple similarities between vehicle and tenor. A good example comes from Milton's *Paradise Lost*, where Satan rises from his stupor and summons all the other fallen devils, lying in heaps around him in the burning floods of hell:

> [*Satan*] stood and called
> His legions, angel forms, who lay entranced,
> Thick as autumnal leaves that strew the brooks
> In Vallombrosa [*a valley in Italy*], where th'Etrurian shades
> High overarched embower; or scattered sedge
> Afloat, when with fierce Winds Orion armed
> Hath vexed the Red Sea coast . . .
> . . . so thick bestrewn,

Abject, and lost, lay these [*i.e. the devils*], covering the flood,
Under amazement of their hideous change.

(Milton, 1998, 1.300–13)

This passage starts in hell, but then soars off first to Italy and
next to the Red Sea, all in the space of a sentence, before
returning us to the situation actually at hand. Like the leaves,
the devils are numerous, fallen and lying still; multiple comparisons within one simile.

Epyllion

An epyllion is a short epic poem. In the Renaissance, when
this became a popular form, epyllia were invariably concerned with love affairs, usually doomed ones. Good examples are Shakespeare's *Venus and Adonis* and Marlowe's *Hero
and Leander*.

Humanist

'Humanist' was the term used to describe those early
sixteenth-century scholars who first sought to resurrect classical learning (this is where the term 'Renaissance', meaning
literally 'rebirth', comes from) by studying classical authors,
and where necessary correcting texts which had become
corrupted. The term reflects the fact that these scholars
were essentially more interested in human affairs than in
divine. The way in which many humanists looked to pagan
philosophers for moral guidance led to tensions with the
Church.

Hyperbole

Hyperbole means deliberate exaggeration, and was a
popular rhetorical effect in the Renaissance period. Many
of the standard images of Petrarchan poetry depended on
hyperbolic statement: the lover weeps so much over his
unrequited love for his lady that his tears could drown a
corn field, while she in turn has eyes like suns or teeth like
pearls.

Iambic pentameter

A line of iambic pentameter has five feet, each made up of an unstressed syllable followed by a stressed one, though it was acceptable and indeed normal for some lines to offer slight variations on this, particularly in the form of a reversal of the pattern (a stressed syllable followed by an unstressed one, known as a trochee) in the first foot of the line or a 'weak' extra syllable in the last one. A good example of a perfectly regular line of iambic pentameter is the first line of Shakespeare's Sonnet 12, 'When I do count the clock that tells the time', where the stressed syllables are clearly 'I', 'count', 'clock', 'tells' and 'time' and the unstressed ones are 'When', 'do', 'the', 'that' and 'the'. (Part of the point is, of course, that the regularity of the line imitates the regular movement of the clock.) A fine instance of a line beginning with a trochee is the opening of *Richard III*, 'Now is the winter of our discontent', where the stress is on the first syllable of the line, 'Now', rather than the second, 'is', and an example of a 'weak' eleventh syllable is 'To be or not to be, that is the question'.

Pastoral

Pastoral writing is set in the countryside, which is described there in idealized terms as an unspoilt paradise. Pastoral is now, however, what would now be called nature writing: it displays a consciously artificial, highly artful version of the countryside. Pastoral writing can take many forms – poetry, prose or drama – but is particularly associated with the 'eclogue', a short verse conversation between two speakers. Pastoral is defined and discussed more fully in Chapter 2 of this book.

Petrarchan

The Italian poet Francesco Petrarca (1304–74) wrote love poems to a beautiful but unattainable woman whom he named Laura. It is not clear whether she ever existed or was a fictional construct, but the formula which Petrarch developed was hugely influential and spawned a widespread vogue for love poetry addressed to chaste, aloof, idealized women.

Romance

'Romance', like 'conceit', is another term which might put modern readers on the wrong track because of its apparent familiarity. However, to Renaissance readers and audiences a romance meant not particularly a love story but a long story, often but not always in verse, recounting the usually fantastic and sometimes magical adventures of a hero, perhaps someone taken from the Arthurian cycle or some other collection of myths or legends, and often including a pastoral element. Interesting examples are Robert Greene's *Pandosto*, which Shakespeare used as a source for *The Winter's Tale*, or Thomas Lodge's *Rosalynde*, which lies behind *As You Like It*, but the finest romance of the period, and by far the most influential, is Sir Philip Sidney's *The Countess of Pembroke's Arcadia*.

Sonnet

A poem with 14 lines, often influenced by and sometimes a direct translation of the works of Petrarch, is called a sonnet. Some sonnets, known as 'Petrarchan sonnets' or 'Italian sonnets', are divided into an eight-line octave and a six-line sestet; others, known as 'Shakespearean sonnets' or 'English sonnets', consist of three four-line quatrains and a rhyming couplet. Many Renaissance poets produced sonnet sequences – groups of related sonnets, usually tracing the course of a love affair – of which the most notable is Sir Philip Sidney's *Astrophil and Stella*, which tells the story of Astrophil (Sidney) and his hopeless love for Stella (Penelope Rich, sister of the Earl of Essex).

Tragicomedy

Unlike the well-established genres of comedy and tragedy, for which there was classical warrant and a clear generic blueprint, tragicomedy was a new and somewhat problematic form. The formula to which it worked has been well described as 'The danger not the death': the tone is sufficiently serious for audiences to believe at times that a tragic outcome is possible, but ultimately a comic resolution will be provided, even if its fragility is obvious. Shakespeare's 'last plays' have some affinities with tragicomedy, but the masters of the genre were Beaumont and Fletcher, with *Philaster* and *A King and No King* being particularly fine examples.

Translatio imperii

This was the idea that the cultural authority of Troy and Rome had been ultimately transferred to England via Brutus, great-grandson of the Trojan refugee Aeneas, who had allegedly travelled to Britain and named it after himself. Along with the idea of the *translatio imperii* traditionally went the analogous idea of the *translatio studii*, the transfer of knowledge and letters from the classical to the modern world.

Further Reading and Resources

PRIMARY TEXTS

Notes on quotations

All quotations from primary texts have had spelling and punctuation modernized. All texts cited from editions dated 1700 or earlier have been cited from the facsimiles of those editions on the subscription service *Early English Books Online* (http://eebo.chadwyck.com). Plays are cited by act/scene/line number; *The Faerie Queene* is cited by book/canto/stanza number; all other books are cited by page number.

Beaumont, Francis, and John Fletcher. *Beaumont and Fletcher's Plays*, ed. G. P. Baker (1911; London: Dent, 1953).

Cavendish, Margaret. *Natures Pictures Drawn by Fancys Pencil to the Life* (London: J. Martin, 1656).

Donne, John. Poems are cited from ed. Helen Gardner, *The Metaphysical Poets* (Harmondsworth: Penguin, 1961).

Ferguson, Margaret, Mary Jo Salter and Jon Stallworthy, eds, *The Norton Anthology of Poetry*, fourth edition (New York: W. W. Norton, 1996).

Harvey, Gabriel. *Pierce's Supererogation or a New Praise of the Old Ass.* (London: John Wolfe, 1593).

Jonson, Ben. *Ben Jonson*, ed. C. H. Herford, P. Simpson and E. Simpson (Oxford: Clarendon Press, 1925–52).

Lyly, John. *Euphues. The Anatomie of Wit* (London: Gabriel Cawood, 1578).

Marlowe, Christopher. *The Plays of Christopher Marlowe*, ed. Roma Gill (Oxford: Oxford UP, 1971).

Milton, John. *Paradise Lost*, ed. Alistair Fowler, second edition (London: Longman, 1998).

Moulsworth, Martha. *'My Name Was Martha': A Renaissance Woman's Autobiographical Poem*, ed. Robert C. Evans and Barbara Wiedemann (West Cornwall, CT: Locust Hill Press, 1993).

Nashe, Thomas. *The Works of Thomas Nashe*, ed. R. B. McKerrow, rev. F. P. Wilson, five volumes (Oxford, 1958).

Olaus Magnus, *Description of the Northern Peoples [1555]*, trans. Peter Fisher and Humphrey Higgens (London: The Hakluyt Society, 1996).

Purchas, Samuel. *Purchas his pilgrimage. Or Relations of the world and the religions observed in all ages and places discovered, from the Creation unto this present* (London: William Stansby, 1613).

Shakespeare, William. *The Norton Shakespeare*, ed. Stephen Greenblatt, Walter Cohen, Jean E. Howard, and Katherine Eisaman Maus (New York: Norton, 1997).

Sidney, Sir Philip. *Sir Philip Sidney*, ed. Katharine Duncan-Jones (Oxford: Oxford University Press, 1989).

———. *The Countess of Pembroke's Arcadia*, ed. Katherine Duncan-Jones (Oxford: Oxford University Press, 1985).

Spenser, Edmund. *The Faerie Queene*, ed. A. C. Hamilton (London: Longman, 1977).

Spenser, Edmund. *A view of the present state of Ireland* (Dublin: Society of Stationers, 1633).

Strachey, William. *The Historie of Travell into Virginia Britania* (1612), ed. Louis B. Wright and Virginia Freund (London: The Hakluyt Society, 1953).

T. E., *The Lawes Resolution of Women's Rights* (London: John More, 1632).

Webster, John. *The White Devil*, ed. John Russell Brown (Manchester: Revels, 1996).

Webster, John. *The Duchess of Malfi*, ed. John Russell Brown (Manchester: Manchester UP, 1974).

Yates, James. *The castell of courtesie* (London: John Wolfe, 1582).

SECONDARY TEXTS

Belsey, Catherine. *The Subject of Tragedy* (London: Methuen, 1985). Influential book on subjectivity in early modern tragedy.

Bevington, David M. *From Mankind to Marlowe: growth of structure in the popular drama of Tudor England* (Cambridge, MA: Harvard University Press, 1962). Offers a frame for reading sixteenth-century theatre.

Boose, Lynda E. ' "The getting of a lawful race" ': Racial discourse in early modern England and the unrepresentable black woman', in *Women, 'Race' and Writing in the Early Modern Period*, eds Margo Hendricks and Patricia Parker (London: Routledge, 1994), pp. 35–54. On race in the early modern period.

Braunmuller, A. R., ed. *The Cambridge Companion to English Renaissance Drama* (Cambridge: Cambridge University Press, 1990). Useful all-round account of the field.

Briggs, Julia. *This stage-play world: English literature and its background 1580–1625* (Oxford: Oxford University Press, 1983). Excellent one-volume portrait of Elizabethan England.

Callaghan, Dympna. "Othello Was A White Man": Racial Impersonation on the Renaissance Stage', in Hawkes (1996), pp. 192–215.

Carey, John. *John Donne: Life, Mind, and Art* (London: Faber, 1981). The best single-volume book on Donne.

Cheney, Patrick, ed. *The Cambridge Companion to Christopher Marlowe* (Cambridge: Cambridge University Press, 2004). A series of essays offering readings of all parts of the Marlowe canon.

Dollimore, Jonathan. *Radical Tragedy: Religion, Ideology and Power in the Drama of Shakespeare and His Contemporaries* (Brighton: Harvester, 1983). An influential and lively reading of the political potential of early modern drama.

Dollimore, Jonathan and Alan Sinfield. *political Shakespeare: Essays in Cultural Materialism* (Manchester: Manchester University Press, 1985).

Duxfield, Andrew. 'Modern Problems of Editing: The Two Texts of Marlowe's *Doctor Faustus*', *Literature Compass* 3 (2005). www.Literature-compass.com/viewpoint.asp?section=2 &ref=476

Fernie, Ewan, ed. *Spiritual Shakespeares* (London: Routledge, 2005). New essays reflecting the current interest in Renaissance spirituality.

Fitter, Chris. 'Historicising Shakespeare's *Richard II*: Current Events, Dating, and the Sabotage of Essex'. *Early Modern Literary Studies* 11.2 (September, 2005). http://purl.oclc. org/emls/11-2/fittric2.htm.

Foucault, Michel, trans. Alan Sheridan, *Discipline and Punish: The Birth of the Prison* (Harmondsworth: Penguin, 1991).

Gilman, Ernest B. *Recollecting the Arundel Circle: Discovering the Past, Recovering the Future* (New York: Peter Lang, 2002).

Greenblatt, Stephen. *Renaissance Self-Fashioning from More to Shakespeare* (Chicago, IL: University of Chicago Press, 1980). A classic New Historicist text.

Greenblatt, Stephen. 'Invisible Bullets: Renaissance authority and its subversion, *Henry IV* and *Henry V*', in Dollimore and Sinfield (1985), pp. 18–47.

Hackett, Helen. *Virgin Mother, Maiden Queen: Elizabeth I and the Cult of the Virgin Mary*. (London: Macmillan, 1995). A good entry into the complex world of Elizabethan iconography.

Hadfield, Andrew. *Literature, Travel and Colonialism in the English Renaissance, 1540–1625* (Oxford: Oxford University Press, 1998). A useful survey of one of the most important topics of the period.

Hall, Kim F. *Things of Darkness: Economies of Race and Gender in Early Modern England* (Ithaca, NY: Cornell University Press, 1995). Excellent account of the way blackness is interpreted in the Renaissance.

Happé, Peter, *English Drama before Shakespeare* (London: Longman, 1999).

Hawkes, Terence. *Meaning by Shakespeare* (London: Routledge, 1992). Classic cultural materialist account of the political and other uses that have been made of Shakespeare.

Hawkes, Terence, ed. *Alternative Shakespeares Volume 2* (London: Routledge, 1996).

Hawkes, Terence. *Shakespeare in the Present* (London: Routledge, 2002).

Howard, Jean E. 'Shakespeare, Geography, and the Work of Gender on the Early Modern Stage', *Modern Language Quarterly* 64.3 (2003), pp. 299–302.

Jardine, Lisa. *Still Harping on Daughters: Women and Drama in the Age of Shakespeare* (London: Harvester, 1983).

———. 'Twins and travesties: Gender, dependency and sexual availability in *Twelfth Night*, in *Erotic Politics: Desire on the Renaissance stage*, ed. Susan Zimmerman (London: Routledge, 1992), pp. 27–38.

Kantorowicz, Ernst. *The King's Two Bodies: A Study in Mediaeval Political Theology* (Princeton, NJ: Princeton University Press, 1997).

Leahy, William. 'Propaganda or a Record of Events? Richard Mulcaster's *The Passage Of Our Most Drad Soveraigne Lady Quene Elyzabeth Through The Citie Of London Westminster The Daye Before Her Coronacion.*' *Early Modern Literary Studies* 9.1 (May 2003). http://purl.oclc.org/emls/09-1/leahmulc.html.

Leggatt, Alexander. *English drama: Shakespeare to the Restoration, 1590–1660* (London: Longman, 1988). Follows on neatly from the studies of Bevington and Happé.

Lewis, C. S. *A Preface to 'Paradise Lost'* (London: Oxford University Press, 1942). Elegant and controversial insight into a Renaissance Christian world-view.

Marcus, Leah. 'Marlowe *in tempore belli*', in *War and Words: Horror and Heroism in the Literature of Warfare*, eds Sara Munson Deats, Lagretta Tallent Lenker and Merry G. Perry (Lanham: Lexington Books, 2004), pp. 295–316. Insightful account of Marlowe's continuing political relevance.

Maley, Willy. *Salvaging Spenser: Colonialism, Culture and Identity* (London: Macmillan, 1997).

May, Steven W. 'Tudor aristocrats and the mythical "stigma of print" ', *Renaissance Papers* (1980): pp. 11–15.

Morgan, K. O., ed. *The Oxford History of Britain* (Oxford: Oxford University Press, 1984). One-volume history of Britain since the conquest, worth seeking out for its terse and helpful chapters on the early modern period.

Neill, Michael. *Issues of Death: Mortality and Identity in English Renaissance Tragedy* (Oxford: Oxford University Press, 1997). Excellent book on tragic representations of death.

Norbrook, David. 'Introduction' to H. R. Woudhuysen, ed., *The Penguin Book of Renaissance Verse 1509–1660* (Harmondsworth:

Penguin, 1992). A brief primer for reading the poetry of the whole period.

Norbrook, David. *Poetry and Politics in the English Renaissance*, revised edition (Oxford: Oxford University Press, 2002).

Perry, Maria. *The Word of a Prince: A Life of Elizabeth I* (Woodbridge: Boydell, 1990).

Price, David A. *Love and Hate in Jamestown: John Smith, Pocahontas and the Heart of a New Nation* (London: Faber and Faber, 2004).

Rabkin, Norman. 'Rabbits, Ducks, and *Henry V*'. *Shakespeare Quarterly*, Volume 28, Issue 3 (Summer 1977), pp. 279–296.

Rukeyser, Muriel. *The Traces of Thomas Hariot* (New York: Random House, 1970).

Salzman, Paul. *English Prose Fiction 1558–1700: A Critical History* (Oxford: Clarendon Press, 1985).

Smith, Bruce R. *The Acoustic World of Early Modern England* (Chicago, IL: University of Chicago Press, 1999). Brilliant reconstruction of perceptions of sound in the Renaissance period.

Spiller, Michael R. G. *The Development of the Sonnet: An Introduction* (London: Routledge, 1992). Short book on a single poetic form.

Strong, Roy. *Henry, Prince of Wales and England's Lost Renaissance* (London: Thames and Hudson, 1986).

Tennenhouse, Leonard. *Power on display: the politics of Shakespeare's major genres* (New York: Methuen, 1986).

Tillyard, E. M. W. *The Elizabethan World-Picture* (Harmondsworth: Penguin, 1972).

Waller, Gary. *English Poetry of the Sixteenth Century*, second edition (London: Longman, 1993).

Wimsatt, W. K. and Monroe C. Beardsley. 'The Intentional Fallacy', in W. K. Wimsatt, *The Verbal Icon: Studies in the Meaning of Poetry* (Lexington, KY: Kentucky University Press, 1954).

Young, Robert V. *Doctrine and Devotion in Seventeenth-Century Poetry: Studies in Donne, Herbert, Crashaw, and Vaughan* (London: Boydell and Brewer, 2000).

ELECTRONIC RESOURCES

Electronic resources give today's students of Renaissance literature tools that their predecessors never had. Texts and criticism, previously impossible to get hold of are now only a matter of seconds away and can be searched in ways that would previously have been impossibly time-consuming. Any serious student of Renaissance literature should be looking to make expertise in electronic resources an essential part of their scholarly toolkit. While the fast-changing nature of electronic resources means that advice about them is always in danger of being out-of-date, here is an annotated list of what we consider to be, currently, the most important resources in the field. All of the resources below are accessible through an internet browser.

Subscription

If your university subscribes to these, they are well worth spending time getting to know. If your institution doesn't, ask them if they have any plans to subscribe to them.

http://eebo.chadwyck.com *Early English Books Online*. Page images of every page of almost every book printed in England before 1700. Absolutely foundational.

http://lion.chadwyck.co.uk *Literature Online*. A fully searchable collection of electronic texts covering, among other things, almost all Renaissance poetry and drama, and an increasing amount of prose. Also has a very full and useful bibliography of criticism, searchable, and containing an increasing number of full-text scholarly journals.

www.oed.com *The Oxford English Dictionary*. The industry standard dictionary, the biggest and the best by far. Use its illustrative quotations to explore the flavour of individual words, and how they change over time.

www.oxforddnb.com *The Oxford Dictionary of National Biography*. Contains authoritative biographical accounts of 50,000 British historical figures, including writers from Shakespeare to the most minor of minor poets, and pretty much anyone with any claim to fame in Renaissance England.

http://muse.jhu.edu *Project Muse.* Full-text access to electronic versions of a number of current scholarly journals.

Non-subscription

Search engines

There are many different search engines, and since they're so important it's worth finding out a bit about how they work. Search Engine Watch, www.searchenginewatch.com, provides a good guide to what search engines are out there, and to which indices they use. At the time of writing, the leading search engine is www.google.com, although when Google can't find what you're after, it's worth trying rivals including www. yahoo.com and www.teoma.com, as they're actually based on different sets of information about what can be found on the Internet.

Remember, search engines look for documents containing the specific words you've typed in: so a search for **critical discussions of why Ferdinand becomes a werewolf** will find that phrase, not such discussions. The three words **Webster, Ferdinand, werewolf** give you much better results. You can use the symbol '' to search for a specific phrase and the minus sign to exclude unwanted words (for example, a search for **"John Ford"-western** is a good way to start to distinguish John Ford the dramatist from his namesake the film director).

Remember, too, that there is no guarantee that pages found by search engines are of any authority. As a rule of thumb, pages coming from universities (e.g. with addresses ending in .edu or .ac.uk) might have a better claim than pages coming from a site called, for the sake of argument, www.marlowewasamartian.com. Also, at sites with names like www.nohassleessays.com, you'll read student essays, often put online as part of a scheme involving selling essays to unscrupulous failing students. If you're reading this book, your work is likely to be of better quality than theirs, and such essays do not constitute a valid reference point in your own work.

Favourite sites

The following sites are among the authors' favourites. You can
check them out directly, or you may well find yourself being
referred to them by search engines.

Meta-sites

http://shakepeare.palomar.edu: Mr William Shakespeare and
the Internet. Annotated list of links to resources. An ideal start-
ing-point.

http://andromeda.rutgers.edu/~jlynch/Lit/ren.html: The Renaissance section of 'Literary Resources', Jack Lynch's metasite
of links concerning literary studies.

http://vos.ucsb.edu/: The Voice of the Shuttle. Another metasite, aiming to cover all of humanities, including a section on
Renaissance literature.

E-texts and projects

www.gutenberg.org: Project Gutenberg. A large collection of
electronic texts of mostly old and out-of-copyright books.
Check the small print – often you'll find that the e-text is actually a Victorian edition of Jonson, or whoever, that someone
has typed in, which is OK, as long as you bear in mind that
you're using a Victorian, and not a current, edition.

www.bartleby.com: Project Bartleby. Again, full-text tran-
scriptions of slightly out-of-date resources. Particularly useful is
the transcription of *The Cambridge History of English and American
Literature* (originally published in 1907–21), an old-fashioned but
extensive discussion of English literary texts.

www.luminarium.org: Luminarium. A collection of online texts
and links to further resources, with pages on many Renaissance
writers.

darkwing.uoregon.edu/~rbear/ren.htm: Renascence Editions,
an online repository of around 200 works printed in English
between the years 1477 and 1799.

www.geocities.com/litpageadd/moultongeneral.html *Moulton's
Library of Literary Criticism*. An eminently useful transcription of an
anthology of early critics' reactions to, in particular, Shakespeare.

Very good as a repository of old-fashioned remarks. If, for instance, you want to find a nineteenth-century critic arguing that Ophelia is a luminous representative of helpless womanhood, this is a good place to go.

www.newadvent.org/cathen: The Catholic Encyclopedia. Transcribes *The Catholic Encyclopedia* (1913), another dated but massive resource for details on anything theological.

http://ise.uvic.ca: Internet Shakespeare Editions. A pioneering work-in-progress preparing a comprehensive online edition of Shakespeare. The site also contains extensive supporting resources and links.

www.it.usyd.edu.au/~matty/Shakespeare/test.html: Matty Farrow's Shakespeare concordance. One of many Shakespeare concordances available on the Internet, this is a tool which enables you to quickly search the works of Shakespeare for particular words.

shakespeareauthorship.com: The Shakespeare Authorship page, 'dedicated to the proposition that Shakespeare wrote Shakespeare'. A lot of Internet sites raise conspiracy theories in the hope of reattributing the works of Shakespeare to someone more romantic, and in this site David Kathman and Terry Ross give a definitive explanation of why these theories are untenable, and of how we know what we do know about Shakespeare.

Online journals

http://purl.org/emls: *Early Modern Literary Studies*, an online peer-reviewed e-journal.

www.hull.ac.uk/renforum: *Renaissance Forum*, an electronic journal of early modern literary and historical studies.

http://eserver.org/emc: *Early Modern Culture*, an electronic seminar.

Discussion lists

You don't need to join a discussion list to benefit from it – the following lists, which are merely particularly good examples of a wider practice, all have searchable archives of previous discussions. If you do decide to apply to join a list, and you're accepted, bear in mind that you should only ask questions of it once you've exhausted all the more conventional ways of finding out the information you're after.

www.shaksper.net: SHAKSPER, an online conference for all matters Shakespearean.

www.english.cam.ac.uk/sidney/list.htm: SIDNEY-SPENSER, devoted, as the name suggests, to discussion of Sidney and Spenser.

www.urich.edu/~creamer/milton: MILTON-L, a listserv devoted to discussion of John Milton.

REFERENCING

First, an important warning: be careful at all times to maintain a distinction between, on the one hand, notes made by cutting and pasting from electronic resources and, on the other hand, the rough draft of your essay. If sentences pasted from an electronic resource end up in your essay not properly acknowledged as quotations, you will be disciplined for plagiarism.

In the same way as with conventional paper resources, the question to be asked when referencing is: have I given information that describes the source I have actually looked at, and enables someone else to retrace my steps? A good test is to give your essay to a colleague, and to ask them to see if they can check the quotations on the web pages you've actually quoted from. While most university English departments have their own preferred and specified standards, here is one illustrative general-purpose example, giving a source for Steve Roth's argument about the chronology of *Hamlet*:

> Roth, Steve. 'Hamlet as The Christmas Prince: Certain Speculations on *Hamlet*, the Calendar, Revels, and Misrule.' *Early Modern Literary Studies* 7.3 (January, 2002): 5.1–89 <URL: http://purl.oclc.org/emls/07-3/2RothHam.htm>, consulted 1 October 2005.

You'll see that this quotation gives the author name and the page title, the name of the site it was from (and, because this particular site is an e-journal, the issue of the e-journal) and the date it was consulted. Indeed, apart from the date, this description is taken from the e-journal's own description of the article, its contents and its URL.

Index